C. R. GILLESPIE
BSc.,
UNIT
KING
DERB

Drink and c

Longman Applied Psychology
General Editor: Philip Feldman

Biofeedback in practice
Douglas Carroll

The social creation of mental illness
Raymond Cochrane

Psychological aspects of pregnancy
Anthony Reading

Compulsive gamblers
Mark G. Dickerson

Drink and drinking problems
Clive Eastman

Forthcoming:

Chemical control of behaviour
Steven Cooper

The Clinical psychology of old age
A. D. M. Davies and A. G. Crisp

Behavioural medicine
P. G. Harvey and B. Dodd

Methods of changing behaviour
Andrée Liddell

The schizophrenias
M. J. Birchwood, S. Hallet and M. C. Preston

Fears and anxieties
D. C. Rowan and C. Eayrs

Institutional care and rehabilitation
Geoffrey Shepherd

Drink and drinking problems

Clive Eastman

Longman
London and New York

Longman Group Limited
Longman House, Burnt Mill, Harlow
Essex CM20 2JE, England
Associated companies throughout the world

Published in the United States of America
by Longman Inc., New York

First published 1984

British Library Cataloguing in Publication Data
Eastman, Clive
    Drink and drinking problems. – (Longman
    applied psychology)
    1. Alcoholism
    I. Title
    362.2'92   HV5035

ISBN 0-582-29608-0

Library of Congress Cataloging in Publication Data
Eastman, Clive, 1938–
    Drink and drinking problems.

    (Longman applied psychology)
    Bibliography: p.
    Includes index.
    1. Drinking of alcoholic beverages. 2. Alcoholism.
3. Alcoholism – Treatment. I. Title. II. Series.
HV5035.E18   1984   362.2'92   84–5655
ISBN 0–582–29608–0

Set in 9½/11 pt Linotron 202 Times
Printed in Hong Kong
by Wing Lee Printing Co Ltd

Contents

Editor's preface

In most areas of applied psychology there is no shortage of hardback textbooks many hundreds of pages in length. They give a broad coverage of the total field but rarely in sufficient detail in any one topic area for undergraduates, particularly honours students. This is even more true for trainees and professionals in such areas as clinical psychology.

The Longman Applied Psychology series consists of authoritative short books each concerned with a specific aspect of applied psychology. The brief given to the authors of this series was to describe the current state of knowledge in the area, how that knowledge is applied to the solution of practical problems and what new developments of real-life relevance may be expected in the near future. The twelve books which have been commissioned so far are concerned mainly with clinical psychology, defined very broadly. Topics range from gambling to ageing and from the chemical control of behaviour to social factors in mental illness.

The books go into sufficient depth for the needs of students at all levels and professionals yet remain well within the grasp of the interested general reader. A number of groups will find their educational and professional needs or their personal interests met by this series: professional psychologists and those in training (clinical, educational, occupational, etc.); psychology undergraduates; undergraduate students in other disciplines which include aspects of applied psychology (e.g. social administration, sociology, management and particularly medicine); professionals and trainee professionals in fields outside psychology, but which draw on applications of psychology (doctors of all kinds, particularly psychiatrists and general practitioners, social workers, nurses, particularly psychiatric nurses, counsellors – such as school, vocational and marital, personnel managers).

Finally, members of the general public who have been introduced to a particular topic by the increasing number of well-informed and well-presented newspaper articles and television programmes will be able to follow it up and pursue it in more depth.

Philip Feldman

Acknowledgements

I wish to extend my thanks to the following individuals for the parts they played during the preparation of this book. Ada for her encouragement when the writing had slowed to a stop. Bert for his newspaper cuttings. Dorrie for introducing me to Wales. Sue Garvey, Barbara Hudson, Beverley Humphries and Jayne Lloyd for deciphering my writing and typing the final version of the manuscript. Phil Feldman for suggesting the project in the first instance. To the above and to those I have inadvertently omitted from the list I offer my grateful thanks.

Chapter 1

Is there a 'drinking problem' in society?

Historical background

Alcohol was drunk for enjoyment in the Mesopotamia of some 5,000 years ago, whilst hostelries existed there less than 1,000 years later. Indeed, it was in the cuneiform writing of Mesopotamia that drunken behaviour was first recorded, together with a cure for hangover. According to Wilkins (1974) alcohol is mentioned over 200 times in the Old Testament, the ill effects of drinking accounting for about one-fifth of those references. Amongst the many activities with which the Romans diverted themselves, feasting and drinking played major parts. It is probably less well known that they introduced one of the earliest methods of discouraging excessive drinkers. The unfortunate patient was forced to drink from a wine cup that contained an eel. Rather more recently, Ghenghis Khan instructed his troops that they should restrict themselves to no more than a single drunken episode per week (Roueche 1960).

In Britain, during the reign of Queen Anne (1665–1714), drunkenness was rife amongst all classes of society, although this seems to have been a male prerogative. Inebriated magistrates appeared on the bench whilst Court Martials were restricted to sitting only before dinner. Both ale and wine were drunk by the rich, whilst the poor were restricted to ale and the new tipple of cheap, inferior spirits.

The heyday of cheap gin, of Hogarth's 'Gin Lane', occurred in the reign of George II (1683–1760). Control was eventually exercised over this lethal trade by the Act of 1751, in which spirits were heavily taxed, and their retailing more narrowly restricted (Trevelyan 1944). However, alcohol provided one of the few means of psychological escape from the miserable, grinding poverty and sweated labour that characterized the lower strata of Victorian society. The demand for cheap alcohol was readily met by the suppliers, and public drunkenness was common. The licensing of premises to retail alcohol became mandatory in Britain as recently as 1914. Concurrently, restrictions were placed on the times during which drink could be sold and drunk on those premises, hence 'licensing hours' were established.

It is clear from this brief account that, historically, drinking problems have always existed in society. The question is whether a widespread drinking problem still exists in contemporary society, or is that a thing of the past? This question is not as simple to answer as it may appear at first sight. Two questions are involved; not one. First, what is the public perception of drinking problems and, second, what is the empirical evidence? It is to these questions that we now turn.

Drinking problems in society: a commonsense view

What might the 'average' person's view be of the prevalence of drinking problems? My own unsystematic enquiries have revealed a number of recurrent themes, some of which warrant brief mention. The most frequent response to my inquiries was that, since most drinkers do not experience drink-related problems, there is obviously no very great contemporary drinking problem. My informants also pointed out that drinking alcohol is a widespread and well-established social custom that gives much pleasure to many people. The 'average' drinker is likely to go 'over the top' only at celebrations, but this is well understood and condoned by most people. Habitual over-indulgence is a problem for a minority of weak-willed people, although the average person cannot understand how anyone can reach such a pass. The only experience that most people have with drink-associated problem behaviour concerns the occasional contact with drunken football supporters, a glimpse of a vagrant alcoholic, a pub brawl, and knowing of someone who habitually drinks too much.

Fortunately, there are some recent systematic data concerning people's perceptions of their own drinking, and of drinking problems. Wilson (1980a) carried out a survey on behalf of the Department of Health and Social Security, in which a random sample of nearly 2,000 people were interviewed. Amongst the many findings, it was shown that both sexes tended to describe themselves as being lighter drinkers than their reported consumption would indicate. Indeed, only 11 per cent of the male, and 15 per cent of the female heavy drinkers described themselves as such. The majority of the sample, 63 per cent, were aware of an increase in the number of problem drinkers over the previous ten years. Some 80 per cent believed that young people under 21 were drinking more than was the case ten years previously, whilst only 48 per cent recognized that adults were also drinking more. In each of these cases, a higher proportion of the female respondents were aware of the true situation.

Drinking problems in society: the true situation

Excessive alcohol intake is associated with a range of physical, psychological, economic, occupational, familial, interpersonal and social problems. Of those mentioned below, some will receive greater attention in subsequent chapters.

Physical problems

It is widely known that excessive drinking over a number of years can lead to liver damage. Cirrhosis, although not the only type of liver disease, is an extremely unpleasant and serious condition in which the normal substance of the liver is replaced by fibrous tissue. Cirrhosis is associated with a much elevated mortality rate. Some studies have shown that alcoholics have more than ten times the probability of dying from cirrhosis than moderate drinkers. Population surveys have indicated that liver disease is more likely among those in occupations involving contact with alcohol. Much evidence has suggested a strong association between the average consumption of alcohol in a country and the deaths from cirrhosis. Despite the fact that alcoholic liver disease is more common amongst males than females, it is usually more severe in the latter. Thus, women appear to be particularly at risk of developing the more serious forms. Liver disease is not inevitably a consequence of excessive drinking, but excessive drinkers are more prone to liver disease. While it is difficult to say, with accuracy, what constitutes 'excessive' drinking, it appears that the risk of developing cirrhosis is increased in those whose regular daily intake is equivalent to 5–10 pints (3–5½ litres) of beer. Notice that the 'reasonable' maximum, regular, daily consumption of alcohol suggested by the Special Committee of the Royal College of Psychiatrists (1979) is equivalent to 4 pints (2 litres) of beer, or one bottle of wine, or four double measures of spirits.

The pancreas produces pancreatic juice, which is vital for proper food digestion, and the hormone insulin, which enables the muscles and other structures to take sugar from the blood stream. Pancreatitis, an inflammation of the pancreas, is sometimes associated with elevated alcohol consumption. It may be acute or chronic and, when acute, usually involves vomiting and a sudden onset of severe pain in the upper abdomen. It is interesting that pancreatitis is showing a marked increase in young males, a section of the community in which heavy drinking is relatively common. About one-tenth of those suffering from acute pancreatitis die as a consequence.

It is common enough knowledge that those with stomach and duodenal ulcers should severely curtail their alcohol intake, or should abstain entirely. Likewise, it is unwise to drink alcohol when suffering from gastritis or 'indigestion'. It is maybe less widely appreciated that heavy alcohol consumption is associated with peptic ulcers. About one-fifth of all alcoholics have a high probability of contracting such ulcers. Likewise, the miseries of gastritis are familiar to many, if not all alcoholics, just as an 'upset stomach' is sometimes present in normally moderate drinkers as part of the 'morning after' syndrome.

Blood disorders of various kinds can result from the habitual heavy consumption of alcohol, including macrocytosis. This abnormal enlargement of the red cell size is a highly characteristic feature of the blood in pernicious anaemia, and anaemia is sometimes present in those who engage in heavy continuous drinking.

Alcoholics may exhibit symptoms resulting from damage to their central and peripheral nervous system. They may, in other words, show signs of neurological damage, the cause of which is often due to malnutrition, as opposed to any direct attack on the nervous system by the alcohol. Diffuse damage to the peripheral nerves, particularly in the legs, is known as peripheral neuritis or peripheral neuropathy. This condition involves both the motor nerves, those that control movement, and the sensory ones, those that relay sensory information to the brain. The distribution of damage is symmetrical, so that both legs are involved and, when the arms are also affected, both are also afflicted. The symptoms of peripheral nerve damage characteristically involve severe pain, tenderness, a burning sensation, weakness and great difficulty in walking.

Brain damage may occur in those who have been drinking very heavily over many years. Such damage can express itself in several ways. For instance, in Korsakoff's psychosis, recent memory is grossly impaired while distant memory remains relatively intact. In contrast, in alcoholic dementia there is a general global impairment of intellectual functioning. Both conditions are striking to the observer. Some alcoholics develop epilepsy, while excessive alcohol consumption and alcoholism are factors in a sizeable proportion of all head injury cases that present themselves at hospital.

Alcohol can pass from a mother's bloodstream into the bloodstream of her unborn child via the placenta or 'afterbirth'. There is no good reason to believe that harm comes to the foetuses of mothers who drink moderately, but there is an accumulation of evidence that foetal damage may occur in mothers who drink excessively. Damage of this type is referred to as the 'foetal alcohol syndrome'. This may involve abnormalities such as congenital heart disease, cleft palate, an unusually small head, a variety of physical deformities, and mental handicap.

Psychological, social and financial problems

Suicide is very much more prevalent among alcoholics than in the general population. A very rough estimate would indicate that alcoholics are from five to twenty times more likely to commit suicide than their non-alcoholic peers.

Sexual problems are common amongst alcoholics. Typically this manifests itself as an orgasmic dysfunction in women, in which orgasm is unattainable. In men, the impairment is one of impotence, or 'erectile dysfunction' in which an erection is either unattainable or, if attained, it cannot be sustained. Thus, although the male's sexual desire may be stimulated by alcohol, he will lack the ability to satisfy that desire. As the porter expresses it in *Macbeth*: '. . . it [alcohol] provokes the desire, but it takes away the performance . . .' It is probable that although a non-orgasmic woman may be able to engage in sexual intercourse, and even conceal her dysfunction from her partner, these options are not available to the impotent male. Erectile dysfunction is difficult to conceal from one's partner, thus many alcoholics, and excessive drinkers, avoid sexual intercourse. Inevitably, this is likely to produce or exacerbate marital disharmony which, in turn, has major implications for family life. There are likely to be few exceptions to the general rule that an alcoholic in the family disrupts, to a greater or lesser extent, the smooth functioning of that family. Child neglect is probably inevitable when both parents are excessive drinkers, and it is generally believed that child abuse is more likely with such parents. When only one parent is afflicted, child neglect and abuse may be prevented by the other spouse.

It is a fact of life that the non-alcoholic family members attempt to conceal the fact that there is an alcoholic, or excessive drinker, in their family. Typically, such a family rarely entertains visitors, for fear that the 'truth' will be revealed. Friends of the family who know about the drinking problem are likely to avoid visiting, for fear of witnessing or precipitating embarrassing incidents. If the children in the family are of an age when they would normally be bringing friends home to share a meal or to play, this does not happen. Again, the object is to keep the unpalatable truth within the family. Thus, the alcoholic status of the family member is kept secret from the rest of the world by means of a family conspiracy of silence and concealment. This is usually the case whether the alcoholic is a parent or offspring. Ultimately, the truth may be impossible to conceal, with the result that the rest of the family may unite to ostracize the alcoholic, or further protect him or her.

Heavy, excessive drinking is expensive for the individual in two senses. The beverage itself is expensive, so that the family finances are usually placed under considerable strain. Heavy, excessive drinking is expensive in the second sense that the drinker may lose time from work and, in consequence, have a smaller net income. In the latter case, the financial strain on the family is two-fold.

The cost to society at large

Excessive drinkers generally have higher absenteeism rates from work, they take more sick leave, and they are involved in more industrial accidents. It is logical to expect that they are less productive and, at the managerial level, are more likely to make unwise decisions when under the influence of alcohol. The true financial cost of excessive drinking is unknown, but estimates have been made. These attempt to encompass the financial costs relating to industry, commerce, the medical services, therapeutic programmes for alcohol abusers, the legal services, the police, traffic accidents, research, and so forth. The total estimated cost to the United States of America in 1971 was $25.37 billion (Royal College of Psychiatrists 1979). Nearer home, a conservative estimate of the cost of 'alcohol misuse' to the economy in England and Wales in 1977–78 was £650 million. These are significant sums of money, even in the context of national finances.

Driving accidents are more likely when the driver has been drinking so that, in Britain, it is currently illegal to drive, attempt to drive, or be in charge of a motor vehicle, on the road or other public place, if there is more than 80 milligrammes of alcohol per 100 millilitres of one's blood (Williams 1976). One effect of alcohol is to impair physical and intellectual performance without these impairments being apparent to the drinker. Indeed, the drunken driver may claim that his or her driving improves after a 'few' drinks. This is just not so. The roadside 'breath test' was introduced in the Road Safety Act 1967. Despite that, there has been a steady increase, since 1968, in convictions for driving, attempting to drive, and being in charge of a motor vehicle with alcohol in the body above the prescribed limit, with 1973–75 being three especially high years. The number of convictions in England and Wales in 1978 was just over 44,000 (Home Office 1979). It is worth bearing in mind that this is the number of successful convictions obtained by the police. We have no idea what the figure would be if all 'drunken drivers' were apprehended and convicted, except that it would be considerably higher.

There is an association between drinking and crime, but that association is far from simple. Alcohol has a 'disinhibiting' effect on the drinker such that the usual personal, social and cultural inhibitions are weakened. Roughly speaking, caution is attenuated by alcohol, while impulsivity is amplified. What might be an easily resisted temptation for the individual when sober may be acted upon after drinking. Thus the individual may be more prone to take risks after drinking or when intoxicated. Much of alcohol-associated crime is of a petty nature and is carried out by those who exhibit relatively low social stability. They have few interpersonal commitments, they drift from one urban centre to another, they do not remain in any job for long, they are likely to be homeless. Unfortunately for the drunken offender of this type, his or her attempts at crime are quite likely to be bungled, and arrest may follow.

Recidivism and imprisonment may become a way of life from which escape is virtually impossible. There is evidence that up to two-thirds of the male prisoners in England and Scotland have serious drinking problems (Royal College of Psychiatrists 1979). Comparisons have been carried out into alcoholism rates between different types of prisoners. When the straightforward drunken offenders are excluded, it is the short-term prisoners who typically exhibit high rates of alcoholism, in contrast to the low rates observed in the long-term incarcerated. An exception to this finding is the high rate of alcoholism found among those serving life sentences (Edwards, Hensman and Peto 1971).

Despite the unacceptably high rates of violent crime in Britain, the social norm against interpersonal violence is observed by the vast majority of people. On the other hand, there can be few who have never experienced the urge to direct violence against some other person. Given the disinhibitory effects of alcohol, it is not surprising to find an association between violent crimes and drinking. What might otherwise have been no more than a minor fracas may escalate into a serious assault or a killing, when one or more of the adversaries is intoxicated. Several studies have led to the conclusion that about half those convicted of murder were intoxicated when they carried out the deed.

Thus far, in this introductory chapter, it has been argued that excessive drinking is associated with a variety of individual, inter-personal, familial, and social problems. While this may be tragic for those involved, the reader may be wondering about the scale of the problem. It is to this question of scale that we now turn.

The epidemiology of drink-associated problems

Epidemiology is the scientific study of the occurrence and distribution of pathology in populations. Before proceeding further, however, the concepts of 'prevalence' and 'incidence' must be defined, since the difference is important. Prevalence refers to the true rate of occurrence in the population at a given time. For instance, if 2 per cent of the population were 'alcoholics', the prevalence of alcoholism would also be 2 per cent. Incidence refers to the rate at which new cases are detected in a population over a given time period. Thus, if one person in one thousand of the population sought, for the first time, treatment for alcoholism during a given time period, the incidence of alcoholism in that population over that time period would be one per thousand, or 0.1 per cent. How does this bear on the epidemiology of drink-associated problems?

First, we cannot directly observe, for example, the

prevalence of drunkenness in a population. The best that can be done is to sample the population, obtaining self-report data. If the sample was truly representative of the population from which it was drawn, and if the self-reports of drunkenness were honest, a good estimate of the prevalence could be determined. Unfortunately, there is considerable regional variation in drinking practices, so a representative sample of the British population is not easy to assemble. People also vary in the extent to which they truthfully report their own drinking practices and intoxication frequencies. Both exaggeration and under-reporting are possible. Even so, surveys of that sort have been carried out, and the results are useful, as long as their limitations are borne in mind. A second difficulty facing epidemiologists is that incidence data are not a true reflection of the total number of new cases that occur in the population over a given time period. By definition, incidence is a measure of the number of new cases that come to light. It follows that incidence data always under-estimate the number of new cases that occur *in the population*. A third difficulty relates to the prevalence data, mentioned above. It will be appreciated that, unless otherwise stated, prevalence data include cases of both long-standing and new pathology. A reduction in preva-lence over a given time period could be the result of fewer new cases, or of some long-standing cases being cured or the individuals moving away from the area under survey, or of them dying. Such a reduction could result from combinations of all four factors. Although other difficulties also apply to interpreting epidemiological data, only one more that is of particular interest in the current context will be discussed. Interpretation of the official data concerning, for instance, 'offences of drun-kenness' involve several of the difficulties mentioned so far, and more besides. In 1978, the total number of offences of drunkenness, in England and Wales, that were proved in court was 106,814. This statistic includes first offenders and recidivists. It also includes cases in which an individual was found guilty on more than one occasion during the year in question. It under-represents the total number of offences of drunkenness that would have led to a finding of guilt, had all been detected, and police proceedings taken. It is important to recall that the police have discretionary powers and are more likely to take proceedings in cases involving violence, or that may or do lead to a breach of the peace, than with cases that cause no such difficulties.

What all this amounts to is that one must treat the epidemiological data with informed caution. Even so, the available statistics make grim reading.

The population of the UK in the 1970s was constant at about 56 million. While incomes rose the percentage of total consumer expenditure on a variety of basic items changed. Thus, between 1968 and 1978 in England and Wales, consumers spent a smaller proportion of their money on food, but more on housing. Over the period 1966–77, the proportion spent on alcohol rose from 6.7 to 7.8 per cent. Over the period 1968–78 there was a virtually uninterrupted increase in the per capita consumption of all alcoholic beverages. A similar trend towards higher per capita alcohol consumption occurred throughout Western Europe.

In 1978, the total number of drunkenness offences that came to the attention of the police was 108,728 with 106,814 court convictions obtained. Both represented a slight reduction over the previous two years. However, between 1970 and 1977, there was an increase in the number of convictions obtained against young people, up to and including 20-year-olds. The increase exceeded 150 per cent for women, compared with more than 60 per cent for men.

Within the age bracket of 14–20 years, the peak age for drunkenness convictions is 18 for males and females. In 1978, 5,759 male 18-year-olds and 356 females were found guilty of drunkenness offences. When all age groups from 14 years upwards are considered, it is the 18-year-old group that has the highest proportion of drunkenness convictions.

In 1968, one year after the introduction of roadside breathalyser testing, 16,752 offences of driving, attempting to drive, and being in charge of a vehicle with a blood alcohol content above the prescribed maximum were proven. A steady increase in convictions took place until the peak year of 1975, when 52,563 such convictions were recorded. The figure in 1978 still stood at an astonishing 44,249. It is salutary to note that, according to the Department of the Environment (1976) in the so-called 'Blennerhassett Report', half the male deaths between the ages of 16 and 24 years result from road accidents; the largest single factor in these accidents being alcohol.

Over the period from 1970–77, psychiatric hospitals and alcoholism units admitted an increasing number of individuals with primary diagnoses of alcoholism or alcoholic psychosis. Increases in female admissions, for all ages, were nearly twice as high as for males, but the largest increase for both males and females was in the less than 25-year-old age group.

Even when full weight is given to the epidemiological problems mentioned above, it is clear that alcohol-related problems are not the sole concern of the excessive drinker and his or her immediate contacts. The scale of drinking problems is so great that it is and must be a national concern. At the level of the individual, excessive drinking is likely to lead to a variety of physical and psychological problems. Sadly, some alcoholic women give birth to babies with congenital physical and intellectual defects; the 'foetal alcohol syndrome'. Alcohol abuse is associated with increased mortality, suicide, and child neglect. Family life and social functioning become impaired, and occupational, financial and social stability are undermined.

In terms of sheer misery, the cost of alcohol misuse is high for the excessive drinker and the family. Friends and colleagues may not totally escape this cost either. Drunken driving may bring total strangers into the sphere of influence of alcohol abuse, just as alcohol-associated crimes may have minimal or maximum consequences for the victims. Unfortunately, the inescapable conclusion to be drawn from the currently available indices is that the problem of alcohol misuse, of 'problem drinking', is increasing, particularly among the young. The scale of the problem at a national level is massive.

Chapter 2

The problems of definition and description

In the previous chapter, terms such as 'alcoholic', 'alcoholism', 'average drinker', 'excessive drinking', and 'problem drinking' were used freely. There is no objection to that, providing the meanings of these terms are well-established and unambiguous.

Regrettably, although these terms are well established, they are open to any number of interpretations. Let us consider just two examples; the terms 'alcoholic' and 'average drinker'. I suggest that you define these terms, then ask two or three other people to attempt the task. Unless all concerned have some prior knowledge of the literature concerning drinking and drinking problems, there are likely to be as many different definitions as there are participants in this exercise. If you are already acquainted with the field, you will know the difficulties resulting from the absence of universal, or even widespread, agreement concerning the definitions of terms that are the common currency of most people working in the field. The 'difficulties' referred to above, arise when different people use the same term to refer to different things, or different terms to refer to the same thing.

The first point, using one word to mean many things, can be illustrated with the familiar term 'alcoholic'. To many people an 'alcoholic' is a vagrant methylated spirits drinker while, to others, 'alcoholic' is synonymous with 'drunkard'.

Some professionals use the term 'alcoholic' to refer only to drinkers who are physically addicted to alcohol, whilst others qualify the term by referring to some well-established definition, as in: 'He is an alcoholic, in the sense of the World Health Organization definition'. As we shall see later, there is a body of opinion that would banish the term from professional thinking, on the grounds that it is irrevocably debased.

The use of different words to refer to the 'same' thing can be illustrated by the terms 'average' and 'moderate' drinker. Is a 'moderate' drinker an 'average' one? An individual can only be defined as an 'average' drinker within a specific context, be it by sex, age, marital status, occupation, region, nationality or whatever. Thus, I may be an average drinker when compared to others of my sex and age, or even sex, age, marital status, occupation, region and nationality. However, I may be an 'excessive' drinker in comparison with some other groups, and a 'light' drinker compared with yet others. Returning to the question: Is a 'moderate' drinker an 'average' one? The answer is 'If that is the way you want it!' The reader will recognize that it all depends on how we define the terms we use.

The term 'average' is a statistical one and can be defined precisely. In consequence, it is possible to identify people whose drinking is 'average' within the sample of which they are a member. Conversely, the term 'moderate' has no precise, universally accepted meaning. If we wish it to have a precise meaning, we have to give it one. If we decide that our 'average' drinker is actually a 'moderate' one then, reciprocally, a 'moderate' drinker is, by definition, one whose drinking corresponds to that of our 'average' drinker. The important point to keep in mind is that we have arbitrarily conferred a particular meaning on the term 'moderate'; a meaning that may not be shared by others. Unless we say what we mean when we refer to 'moderate' drinkers, we are likely to find ourselves talking at cross purposes. The same difficulty arises with the other terms referred to at the start of this chapter.

Before turning to the definitions of words such as 'alcoholic' and 'excessive' drinking, let us look at what may seem to be the simpler problem of describing an individual's drinking pattern.

Drinking patterns

In the above example of the average drinker, I have been guilty of an intentional sleight-of-hand. It was stated that: '. . . it is possible to identify people whose drinking is "average" within the sample of which they are a member'. What did you have in mind when you read that? You may have been thinking about the amount of alcoholic beverage that is consumed, on average. *Quantity* is one important aspect of drinking, but quantity, alone, cannot provide an adequate picture of an individual's drinking. 'He drinks one pint, no more, no less, at a sitting', may appear to describe a 'light' drinker. If we are thinking in terms of beer, many would agree that one pint per session is light drinking. What if the one pint were not beer but brandy? Few would take the view that drinking one pint of brandy at a sitting could be regarded as 'light' drinking. Thus, we need to know how much an individual drinks and what is consumed. This is sometimes expressed in terms of the absolute (100 per cent) alcohol equivalent. The perceptive reader may already realize that this still provides a grossly inadequate picture. Two people may drink no more and no less than one pint of a certain beer at a sitting, but one may drink only once a year while the other drinks twice every day. We need to take the *frequency* of drinking into account.

So far, we have decided that in order to describe an individual's drinking pattern, we need to know what, how much and how frequently that person drinks. This still would not allow one to construct comprehensive descriptions of every drinking pattern. We may know that two people drink the same quantity of the same beverage on the same number of occasions each year. We also need to take into consideration the *distribution*, or patterning, of those occasions throughout the year. One drinker may evenly distribute his or her drinking over the entire year; always drinking in the evening. The other drinker may concentrate, or 'bunch' the drinking in a few periods during the year; always drinking throughout the day.

The reader may feel that we have now gone far enough and can, in consequence, construct a comprehensive description of any drinking pattern. This is not so, although only one additional factor will be mentioned here; that of the *variability* in quantity consumed on different drinking occasions. Some people never vary the amount and sort of beverage they consume in any sitting, while others may drink within quite wide limits. For example, although two individuals may average four pints of beer per sitting, one may achieve this by drinking four pints always, whereas the other may drink one pint on half the drinking occasions and seven pints on the remaining half. Clearly, these are quite different drinking patterns.

To recapitulate, it has been suggested that several factors must be taken into account if drinking patterns are fully to be described. These factors include: quantity, frequency, distribution of drinking occasions, amount consumed (as absolute alcohol equivalent), and variability of the amount consumed. Although this is a long list, already, it still omits some important factors. It does not include information about *where* the drinking occurs, whether it is done in company or in solitude, whether it replaces food, whether it gives rise to intoxication, and so forth. What may originally have appeared to be a simple matter is now, presumably, seen to be complex. It becomes more complex, still, when attempts are made to construct a drinking 'index'. The object of such an exercise is to bring together and represent the factors, by means of which drinking patterns are characterized, in such a way as to make valid comparisons of different patterns easily possible. By far the commonest index in current use is a two-dimensional one: the Quantity–Frequency Index (QF). Typically, various combinations of quantity and frequency are given verbal labels such as: 'light', 'moderate', and 'heavy' drinking. For practical purposes, this is often good enough. Unfortunately, different research workers have tended to use the same verbal labels for different or only partly similar quantity/frequency combinations. The result is that it is often impossible to make simple, direct, comparisons between different studies.

Before leaving the subject of drinking patterns, it is worthwhile considering the distinction between 'abstainers' and 'drinkers'. One's first reaction might be that this distinction is so clear that it is not a problem. Predictably, that is not so. The problem is most clearly recognized when one considers the person who drinks only on 'special occasions' and then takes only a sip. This may occur only once a year, on New Year's Eve for example, or may be only at wedding parties. Is such an individual an abstainer or a drinker? The reader may think that, in the strictest sense, that person is a drinker, but many such 'drinkers' would hotly reject that label. One frequently used criterion is that of whether the individual has consumed any alcohol, whatsoever, in the previous 12 months. Given that yardstick a person could alternate many times between 'abstainer' and 'drinker' during a lifetime.

The general conclusion to be drawn from this section is that it is difficult fully to characterize drinking patterns in ways that permit easy and valid comparisons although, in practice, two- or three-dimensional indices are often adequate for that purpose.

Definitions

Much effort and time has been spent on attempts to

provide precise and generally acceptable definitions for the many terms that are the common currency of all communications concerning drink and drinking problems. One of the most recent and comprehensive accounts was that provided by Keller (1977), and it is that account which provides much of the material in this section. Here, we shall confine ourselves to those definitions that are of particular relevance in the current context.

As I pointed out at the start of this chapter, the terms 'alcoholic' and 'alcoholism' are thought by many professionals to be so debased that they should be scrapped. This is not the place to argue for or against that proposition, but the fact is that these terms are widely used and are unlikely to be abandoned in the foreseeable future. What, then, do the words 'alcoholic' and 'alcoholism' signify?

We shall not consider the many different definitions that have been proposed, since that is unnecessary for our present purposes and would be tedious in the extreme. Here, we shall concentrate on what is probably the most widely accepted definition, together with its proposed replacement. Presumably, it hardly needs to be mentioned that 'alcoholism' is the condition from which 'alcoholics' are said to suffer.

The definition of 'alcoholic' that we shall consider is the one provided by the World Health Organization (WHO) Expert Committee (1952):

> Alcoholics are those excessive drinkers whose dependence on alcohol has attained such a degree that they show a noticeable mental disturbance or interference with their bodily or mental health, their interpersonal relations and their smooth economic functioning, or who show the prodromal signs of such development. They therefore require treatment.

Alcoholism is thus defined in terms of 'excessive' drinking, 'dependence on alcohol', as well as psychological, physical, social and economic impairments. These latter impairments are associated with dependence on alcohol; they are major consequences of that dependence. The three terms upon which I wish to focus are: 'prodromal', 'excessive', and 'dependence'. 'Prodromal' is a medical term signifying the early signs or symptoms of an illness. The implication is that such prodromal manifestations are the precursors or prelude to the full development of the illness. They are warning signs and symptoms. It is interesting to note that the last sentence of the definition refers to 'treatment'. It is plain that the Expert Committee regarded alcoholism as an illness. The word 'excessive' is imprecise, subjective and embodies pejorative implications. Its inclusion in the WHO definition is unfortunate, to say the least, whilst its omission would be a distinct improvement, in my view. Let us now turn to the concept of 'dependence'. The WHO Expert Committee on Addiction-Producing Drugs (1964) defined the concept of dependence, thus:

> A state, psychic and sometimes also physical, resulting from the interaction between a living organism and a drug, characterized by behavioural and other responses that always include a compulsion to take the drug on a continuous or periodic basis in order to experience its psychic effects, and sometimes to avoid the discomfort of its absence. Tolerance may or may not be present. A person may be dependent on more than one drug.

The WHO Committee recommended that 'dependence' should replace the term 'addiction'. Thus, in technical communications, drug 'addiction', regardless of the particular drug 'addiction' involved, is being increasingly superseded by the term drug 'dependence'.

'Tolerance' in the above definition refers to a property that is exhibited by many chemicals that produce altered states of consciousness: the 'psychoactive' drugs. Given an unchanging dose, many such drugs produce less effect when repeatedly administered. The living organism develops a tolerance for the drug, such that increasing amounts of the drug have to be used in order to achieve the effects that, originally, were attainable at much lower doses. This phenomenon is dramatically illustrated in the case of heroin-dependent individuals.

The established heroin 'addict' is eventually able to tolerate a dosage that would have been fatal when he or she first began using the drug. Tolerance does have limits but, in the case of narcotics, the final usual daily dosage may be 20 to 100 times the original level. To a lesser degree, the same phenomenon is observed in alcohol dependence, when a bottle of spirits per day may never give rise to overt intoxication (Office of Health Economics 1981).

Returning to the definition of dependence, above, the term 'compulsion' is important. The concept of 'compulsion', as used here, involves the idea that the dependent drinker experiences a dire need or necessity to drink, if deprived of alcohol, and to continue drinking once started. The compulsion is usually experienced powerfully and to an extent where it 'has' to be acted upon. The heavy smoker experiences a compulsion to smoke when deprived of tobacco. The term 'craving' is often used to describe this subjective experience, in which there is an awareness of impaired personal control over the use of the drug in question. This so-called 'loss of control' phenomenon has been much debated, so it is to this that we now turn.

In 1952 the major figure in the area of alcoholism theorizing and research, E. M. Jellinek, carefully defined the loss of control over drinking concept in a WHO report. He claimed that for those individuals afflicted by this phenomenon, once they have drunk a small amount of alcohol a physical demand for more is experienced. According to this formulation, 'loss of control' refers to the individual's inability to control the amount consumed once the first drink has been taken. Once started, the individual cannot choose to stop. Surprisingly, Jellinek added that the person experiencing the loss of control phenomenon still retains the ability to refrain from taking the first drink. Total abstinence is within their ability, but moderating their intake once started is not. Like Keller (1972) I find it beyond belief that an alcohol-dependent person can consistently control whether or not to drink on a particular occasion.

Accordingly, Keller went on to argue that there are two forms of the loss of control phenomenon, the primary one being a loss of control over whether or not to drink on a particular occasion. The secondary one is a loss of control over whether or not to continue drinking once the first drink has been taken. As Keller was careful to emphasize, there is no suggestion that either form of loss of control is consistently at work. To quote Keller (1972: 162–3):

> the characteristic symptom in alcoholism is that an alcoholic cannot consistently choose whether he shall drink, and if he drinks, he cannot consistently choose whether he shall stop.

If alcohol is withheld from a dependent drinker and if, for whatever reason, there is a sudden reduction in the alcohol level within the body tissues and blood, that person will almost certainly experience 'withdrawal symptoms'. These comprise a 'syndrome' or set of symptoms that usually occur together, although some may be absent on any one occasion. The symptoms may occur within hours or days of drinking, with the milder ones starting earlier. The commonest and earliest manifestation of withdrawal is that of the 'morning shakes'. This includes pronounced tremulousness or shaking of the hands, agitation, restlessness and a feeling of general weakness. Many dependent drinkers experience the shakes every morning, the immediate solution to which is to take a drink. Typically, such a person will explain such early morning drinking as a means of 'steadying my nerves'. It is no exaggeration to say that the physical shaking may be so pronounced that it is difficult to convey the drink to the mouth without spilling most of it. Moderate and severe attacks may include visual and auditory hallucinations.

The most severe withdrawal symptom, and the one of which most people will have heard, is delirium tremens, or the DTs. This usually occurs only in drinkers who have been dependent on alcohol for many years. Kessel and Walton (1965) suggest that the first attack usually occurs after no less than ten years of 'excessive' drinking. The symptoms usually follow a bout of very heavy drinking, and usually commence two to five days after that drinking stops. This severest expression of withdrawal is both dramatic and, in some cases that are not properly cared for, can be fatal. Fully developed, delirium tremens includes gross and continuous tremulousness of the entire body. The afflicted person is extremely agitated and restless, perspiring heavily with a rapid pulse. Utterly confused, the patient experiences terrifying hallucinations believing that he or she is being attacked by hordes of fearsome creatures. Extreme fear is the usual emotional accompaniment of the DTs. The sufferer's response to these symptoms is sometimes aggressive, and sometimes suicidal. If allowed to run its full course, unchecked, the patient emerges completely exhausted. Hospital treatment is aimed at ameliorating the severity and duration of the symptoms and preventing self-destructive behaviour. Despite treatment death sometimes occurs.

The alcohol-dependence syndrome

Although the WHO (1952) definition of 'alcoholic' has served its purpose, it has been strongly criticized for confusing *dependence* with *disability*. There must be many mildly dependent drinkers who have suffered no adverse psychological, physical, social or economic consequences as a result of that dependence. According to the WHO definition, this dependent drinker would not be deemed an alcoholic. It seems that dependence shades into alcoholism only when noticeable disabilities develop.

It has also been objected that the inclusion of medical concepts in the definition, such as 'prodromal' and 'treatment', imply that alcoholism is an illness or disease and that, in consequence, should only be treated by the medically qualified. These terms also imply that alcoholism has its origins in disease, but this is an unproven and highly contentious issue. As a consequence of these and other dissatisfactions with the definition, a new concept, the 'alcohol-dependence syndrome', was advocated in a WHO publication entitled 'Alcohol-related disabilities' (Edwards *et al.* 1977).

The alcohol-dependence syndrome has been proposed in a laudable attempt to break free of much of the conceptual confusion now inherent in the term 'alcoholism'. Crucially, the alcohol-dependence syndrome is distinguished from alcohol-related disabilities. Of probably equal importance is the recognition, within the defining features of the syndrome, that alcohol dependence exists not as an all-or-nothing condition but in degrees. This is also true of alcohol-related disabilities. Thus, the alcohol-dependence syndrome is defined in terms of psychological and physiological dimensions. Conceptually separate are the alcohol-related disabilities, although the dependence syndrome is frequently associated with alcohol-related disabilities. As Edwards (1977), one of editors of the WHO document, pointed out, the current delineation of the syndrome is provisional, due to the paucity of available knowledge concerning many of its aspects. With these preliminary observations, we can now turn to the syndrome itself.

The diagnostic criteria for the alcohol dependence syndrome are seven in number. The order in which they appear in the following list is not intended to indicate the order in which the various signs and symptoms occur.

1. *Narrowing of the drinking repertoire.* The individual's drinking behaviour exhibits less variability than is present in non-alcohol dependent drinkers. The daily drinking pattern becomes increasingly crystallized,

stereotyped and predictable.

2. *Primacy of drinking over other goals*. A preoccupation with thoughts about drinking, planning the day's drinking and involvement in actual drinking becomes evident. Drink and drinking assume prime importance in the individual's life. All other goals, all ambitions, become subordinated to drinking. Nothing and nobody is more important than drinking.

3. *Subjective awareness of a compulsion to drink*. The drinker recognizes that his or her drinking is getting out of control. There is a reduction of drinking control. Attempts by the individual to limit and control drinking are only temporarily successful.

4. *Tolerance to alcohol increases*. Drinkers with high tolerance levels do not necessarily experience withdrawal symptoms, following a drop in blood alcohol level. It is unclear why tolerant drinkers become subject to withdrawal symptoms.

5. *Experience of withdrawal symptoms*.

6. *Drinking to avoid, or obtain relief from, withdrawal symptoms*. Typically early morning drinking is the method adopted by those who experience withdrawal symptoms following a night's abstinence.

7. *Rapid reinstatement of the syndrome following a period of abstinence*. Alcohol-dependent individuals may remain abstinent for a few weeks with surprising ease. Attempts to drink again, but with control, result in a slide back into the syndrome by mildly dependent drinkers, and a catastrophic return to the former drinking pattern by the severely dependent.

It is worth emphasizing, again, that all seven criteria can exist in varying degrees; they are dimensional. Diagnosis includes assessing the degree to which the symptoms are present, their frequency, duration, and pattern of occurrence.

If research into the alcohol-dependence syndrome establishes the validity of the concept, *and* if it gains wide currency among those currently concerned with alcohol-dependent drinkers, the outmoded concept of 'alcoholism' may be 'retired'. Since alcohol is a dependence-providing drug, and since the alcohol-dependence syndrome may be present to a greater or lesser extent, all who drink should be made aware that no one is immune from sliding into that syndrome. A general understanding of the nature of the syndrome should help those who live with, or who treat, alcohol-dependent drinkers to gain a better view of what assails the sufferer. It should also provide a more realistic insight into what is likely to assist, and what to hinder, attempts to break free from that syndrome. Hopefully, this new conceptualization – the alcohol-dependence syndrome – will prove its value at both theoretical and applied levels. Inevitably, it will be superseded by a more refined successor; but that is the way science progresses.

This review of definitions and descriptions is far from complete; additional ones will be discussed where they occur, in the text.

Terminology

The term 'alcoholism' is used throughout this book. Unless otherwise stated, it signifies the condition exemplified in the WHO definition and the alcohol-dependence syndrome. Likewise, drinkers are variously described as 'light', 'moderate', 'modest', 'heavy', and 'excessive'. Having already discussed some of the problems associated with these terms, it will be understood that they have no fixed meaning. In the current context, 'light', 'moderate' and 'modest' describe drinkers who are unlikely to experience problems consequent upon their drinking. 'Heavy' and 'excessive' indicate drinkers who may develop or may already have developed drinking problems. Thus, the terminology is imprecise, overlapping but convenient for the present purposes.

Chapter 3

Alcohol, beverage strength, production and economics

Alcohol

The generic term 'alcohol' refers to a large group of organic chemical compounds which contain one or more hydroxyl groups. The majority of alcohols are poisonous, and find their use in industry as solvents. The compound in which we are interested is known as 'ethyl alcohol' or 'ethanol'. It is a monohydric primary aliphatic alcohol with the formula C_2H_5OH or CH_3CH_2OH. Alcohol, meaning throughout the remainder of this book ethyl alcohol, is a volatile, flammable liquid that boils at 78.1 °C. It is colourless, has a slightly sweet smell and a strong burning taste. It mixes with water in all proportions and is an effective solvent for many organic compounds. Because its molecules are relatively small, it can quickly pass through the vessel walls and membranes of the body. Likewise, it rapidly infiltrates the body's organs and tissues. Alcohol also has a high calorific value so that, in its usual beverage forms, it can represent a major part of the heavy drinker's nutritional intake.

Alcohol occurs in nature when yeast, carbohydrates and water come together. The carbohydrates, in the form of various sugars, are 'fermented' by the yeast fungi to produce carbon dioxide gas and alcohol. Thus, overripe fruit will eventually go rotten and ferment. The odour is partly due to the presence of alcohol. There are stories from India of elephants becoming drunk, having gorged themselves on fermenting bananas. Home-made jams and marmalade which contain no preservative are subject to fermentation, once the container has been opened and yeast spores have entered. Once the process is underway, the typical sweetish odour is noticeable and masses of tiny gas bubbles can be seen in the preserve. The fact is that a very wide range of plant materials and products can provide the source of sugars from which alcohol is derived. Fermentation will produce alcohol from potato peelings or grapes, from domestic sugar or pulped sugar beet, but there are limits to the 'strength' or 'concentration' of alcohol that can be achieved.

There are two factors that determine the point at which fermentation and, therefore, alcohol production ceases. The yeast dies once the concentration of alcohol reaches about 14 per cent by volume. This proportion of alcohol will only be achieved if there is sufficient sugar present. If there is insufficient sugar, fermentation stops once it has been used up, and the resulting beverage is 'dry'. Eventually the yeast dies because it has no sugar on which to feed. If the fermenting liquid contains excess sugar, fermentation ceases when the alcohol is 'sweet'. This is the way in which 'sweet' and 'dry' wines are made. It was not until quite recently, in about AD 800, that an Arabian alchemist developed the method of distillation for producing higher concentrations of alcohol.

Distillation relies upon the fact that different liquids have different boiling points. Alcohol boils at 78.1 °C and water at 100 °C. Hence, if a solution of alcohol and water is heated to 78.1 °C, the alcohol will boil off leaving the water behind. Separation by distillation is known technically as 'fractionation'. The hot alcohol vapour is led away and condensed to produce an aqueous alcohol solution containing 96 per cent alcohol by weight. Beyond that point, 100 per cent ethyl alcohol is obtainable by further fractionation but only by means of a special technique that need not concern us here.

If alcoholic beverages contained only water, alcohol, tasteless colouring and, in the case of 'sweet' drinks, sugar, there would probably exist no more than a handful of such beverages. The differences between them would be apparent only in terms of 'strength', that is alcohol content, sweetness or dryness, and colour. The reason that this is not how things stand is due to many other constituents that occur in most alcoholic beverages. These constituents are referred to as 'congeners', and include various acetates, aldehydes, ketones, 'higher' alcohols, sugars, minerals, proteins, and vitamins of the B-group. The extent to which they are present varies from beverage to beverage, ranging from 3 g per 100 litres of vodka, to 285 g per 100 litres of bourbon (Royal College of Psychiatrists 1979). Their importance to the drinker is twofold. They play a role in producing 'hangovers' and, more important, they impart the colours and flavours that characterize the multitude of different alcoholic beverages. The connoisseurs of beers, wines or spirits have developed an appreciation of, and ability to make fine discriminations between, complex combinations of congeners. It is the congeners that distinguish the 'great' wines from the everyday supermarket 'plonk'. It is the congeners that enable the expert to differentiate between different vintages of the same wine, between different brandies, ports and so forth. The source of the congeners lie in the materials and processes used in making the beverages.

Measures of beverage 'strength'

So far, in this chapter, the 'strength' of an alcoholic beverage, or the 'concentration' of alcohol in a particular beverage, has been described in terms of the percentage by weight or by volume of alcohol. No doubt the most convenient and rational measure of concentration is in terms of volume. Thus, a beverage containing 40 per cent by volume of alcohol, is one in which every 100 units by

volume of the beverage contain 40 units by volume of
alcohol. Unfortunately, the revenue authorities use the
antiquated 'proof' scale for indicating alcohol concentration. Before the advent of more sophisticated
methods, the strength of any spiritous liqour was tested
with the aid of gunpowder. The test was performed by
soaking a small quantity of gunpowder with the
beverage, and igniting the resulting mixture. If the gunpowder burnt, it was 'proof' that the beverage contained
at least the permitted minimum alcohol content, although
in the event it may have contained considerably in excess
of that level. Proof scales are divided into 'degrees'
which, it should be noted, are not equivalent to percent-
ages. The American proof scale is reasonably simple, in
that one degree proof is equivalent to one-half per cent
by volume of alcohol. One hundred degrees proof on the
American scale is equivalent to 50 per cent by volume of
alcohol. The British scale is not so simple, since 100
degrees proof is equivalent to 57.15 per cent by volume
of alcohol. One example may serve to clarify matters.
Branded British whisky is typically described on the label
as being of 70 degrees proof. This indicates that the
beverage contains 40 per cent by volume of alcohol. On
the American scale, that same whisky would be described
as 80 degrees proof.

Alcohol production

Alcoholic beverages can be divided into two broad
classes. The fermented group have a maximum alcohol
content of about 14 per cent by volume, while the
distilled groups may contain up to 55 per cent. Beers and
wines fall into the first group, spirits and liqueurs into the
second. A third, intermediate, group of 'fortified' or
'dessert' wines includes sherry, port and madeira, for
example. These are made from ordinary fermented wines
by adding to, or 'fortifying' them, with brandy, high-
alcohol content spirit and plant extracts for flavouring.

They typically have alcohol contents of 15–20 per cent. The various beverages have different sources; for example, beers are produced by fermenting brewer's 'wort' (an infusion of malt) which contains hops for flavouring. Wines are produced by fermenting crushed grapes or grape juice while, as noted above, fortified wines contain added spirits. The spirits, brandy, gin, rum, vodka, and whisky, are all obtained by single or double distillation of various fermented materials. Brandy is distilled from grape mash, rum from molasses, vodka from grain, and whisky from barley or corn mash. Gin is obtained by re-distilling a tasteless first distillation. Finally, liqueurs are manufactured by adding flavouring to what is usually a tasteless spirit base.

Having briefly sketched the methods by which various types of alcoholic beverages are produced, it is worth considering the scale of production involved. In 1979, there were approximately 43 million United Kingdom residents who were at least 16 years of age. By dividing the total quantities of beverages sold by the size of the population concerned, the national 'consumption' per head of that population can be calculated. The following (rounded) figures were obtained from the Statistical Handbook for 1979 of the Brewers' Society of the UK. Each person 'consumed' 271 pints (158 litres) of beer, 11 pints (6 litres) of spirits, 17 pints (10 litres) of wine, and 8 pints (4½ litres) of cider. Notice that these are 'notional' quantities, since there are wide variations between people in the amount they would normally drink per annum, not to mention the teetotallers in the population. Thus, some drinkers will greatly exceed and some greatly fall short of the above quantities. An interesting statistic obtained from the 1979, November, edition of the Federation of Alcoholic Rehabilitation Establishments' (FARE) information booklet *Alcohol and Alcoholism Services Now* concerns home brewing. The claim was made that this amounted to 52 million pints of beer. The corresponding figure for home-made wine was not given. This level of do-it-yourself brewing gives a normal 'consumption' of just over one pint per head of the population. It would seem that the brewing industry has little to fear from that area of competition. That is not to say there are no heavy consumers of home-brewed beer; no doubt there are, but there are no data available.

The drink industry, overall, provides employment for a considerable number of people. In 1978, about 103,000 individuals were employed in the industry. No less than 253,000 people were employed in public houses in the same year. The total number of people whose livelihood is, to a greater or lesser extent, involved in producing, wholesaling, packaging, advertising, distributing and re-tailing of alcoholic beverages must represent a sizeable fraction of the total working population. One estimate is that some 700,000 jobs are involved (Office of Health Economics 1981). By implication, a great deal of money must be involved in the drink industry, so it is to this matter that we now turn.

The economics of alcohol

In 1979, the total United Kingdom consumer expenditure on all items amounted to about £115,000 million. Table 1 shows how some of that money was accounted for.

Table 1 UK consumer expenditure — 1979

	Millions of pounds	Percentage of total expenditure
Food	20,505	17.9
Housing	16,501	14.4
Transport, vehicles and other travel	15,440	13.5
Alcohol	8,873	7.7
Fuel and light	5,527	4.6
Tobacco	4,279	3.7

Source: Social Trends 1981

Nearly £9,000 million were spent on alcohol, representing almost 8 per cent of all consumer spending. In the same year, 1979, Custom and Excise Duty plus Value Added Tax (VAT) on that alcohol provided the government with an income of £2,928.1 million (*Brewers' Statistical Handbook 1980*). The current (1982) corresponding government income from alcohol sales is probably in excess of £3,500 million. In addition, the sale of spirits abroad represents an export income to the nation of about £1,000 million (Office of Health Economics 1981). Even by national standards, these are substantial amounts of money.

There is ample evidence that the consumption of alcohol per head of the population (aged 15 years and over) has been rising rapidly over recent years. Table 2(a), based upon data from the *Brewers' Statistical Handbook* for 1981, illustrates this point.

It is worth noting that the 1979 consumption figures are equivalent to more than 17 pints (10 litres) of pure alcohol per head of the population.

These consumption figures can be converted to percentage increases over each decade, as shown in Table 2b.

Table 2(a) Consumption (in pints) per head of the population aged 15 years and over

Year	Beer	Spirits	Wine	Cider
1959	178.5	3.7	4.1	4.0
1969	220.3	4.6	8.6	4.9
1979	270.8	10.7	17.4	8.4

(*b*) Percentage increase in consumption per head of the population aged 15 years and over

Decade	Beer	Spirits	Wine	Cider
1959–69	23.4	24.3	109.8	22.5
1969–79	22.9	130.4	102.3	71.4

The increase in spirits consumption during the latter decade, and the increases in wine drinking over both decades are particularly impressive. Given this trend of increasing alcohol consumption, it is important to understand how it has come about. As with the vast majority of psychological, social, political, economic, industrial and commercial trends, to name but a few, there is no single cause. There may be one major cause but other subsidiary causes also play their part. It follows that many explanations are often possible, depending upon the originator's standpoint. Thus, a psychologist would probably provide an explanation involving psychological concepts, whereas a sociologist would be more concerned with social factors. Each explanation might be valid, but would probably represent no more than a part of the 'total' or 'full' explanation. Unfortunately, the 'full' explanation of any social phenomenon is unlikely ever to be revealed. However, in the present context of alcohol economics, let us seek an economic explanation for the increasing alcohol consumption.

One explanation might be that the increase in alcohol consumption simply reflects a general increase in consumer spending. The following table of consumer expenditure (Table 3(a)) supplies some relevant data on

Table 3(a) Consumer expenditure at constant 1975 prices

Year	Beer	Spirits, wine, cider	All items
1959	1,572	782	43,979
1969	2,188	1,273	56,169
1979	2,808	2,490	68,305

(b) Percentage increases in consumer expenditure at constant 1975 prices

Decade	Beer	Spirits, wine, cider	All items
1959–69	39.2	62.8	27.7
1969–79	28.3	95.6	21.6

this point. In order to make direct comparisons of expenditure, the distorting effects of changes in the 'real' value of money have been eliminated by converting all amounts to their equivalents at constant 1975 prices. The figures refer to million pounds sterling. These figures appear to support our hypothesis, but a different picture emerges when the percentage increases are calculated as shown in Table 2(b).

It can now be seen that although consumer expenditure on all items has been increasing over the two decades from 1959, there has been a much greater relative increase in expenditure on alcohol. Thus, our hypothesis, that the increase in alcohol consumption reflects no more than a general increase in all consumer expenditure is, at best, only a partial explanation. It does not account for the full increase in expenditure on alcohol.

An alternative explanation might concern the relative cost of alcohol when compared to income. The data in Table 4 were taken from an article on Excise Duties by Harris (1982).

Table 4 Prices of whisky and beer compared to contemporary average weekly earnings of male manual workers

	1960	1970	1980
Earnings (£)	14.10	23.0	123.0
Bottle of whisky (£)	1.78	2.80	5.25
Percentage of earnings	12.6	12.2	4.3
Pint of beer (£)	0.06	0.101	0.405
Percentage of earnings	0.4	0.4	0.3

It can be seen that the price of a pint of beer has changed very little relative to weekly income, while the price of a bottle of whisky has fallen dramatically. The table of percentage increase in consumption per head of the population (Table 2b p. 34) shows that beer consumption has increased much less than spirit consumption. Note that the beer consumption increases were pretty well constant over the two decades, as was the price as a percentage of weekly income. The increase in spirit consumption tripled from 1969–79, while the price, as a percentage of weekly income, fell by a factor of three. All this suggests that the reduction in the relative cost of alcohol has resulted in an increase in consumption. This does appear to be a plausible explanation, a conclusion supported by additional information appearing in *The Times* article (Harris 1982). It was pointed out that the recession in Britain has resulted in a reduction in alcohol sales; as disposable incomes have fallen for many people, spending on alcohol has also fallen. Some Scottish distilleries may have to work for only part of the year, and older and less economic breweries are likely to close. These are serious matters even for the drinks industry, which had about £1,700 million of invested capital in 1978. The size of this sum can be gauged from the fact that it was approximately 4.5 per cent of the Gross National Product (GNP) in that year (FARE 1979).

In view of the large capital investment in the drinks industry, and bearing in mind the huge turnover of money resulting from the sale of its products, it is not surprising that there is a large annual investment in advertising. During 1979, four major brewers each spent in excess of £3 million on advertising, while two others spent more than £2 million. These six major brewers spent a total of £17.468 million on advertising in 1979 (Campaign 1980). It is clear that the drinks industry is an important one. It is a major employer, it makes a large contribution to the nation's export trade, it provides an even larger income for the government through Excise Duty and VAT on alcohol, and it spends a great deal of money on advertising its products. Even though it would be grossly unfair to blame the drinks industry for the indubitable fact that some people develop drinking problems, that industry only makes a very small direct financial contribution to research into alcohol abuse. Thus, the

November 1979, FARE publication *Alcohol and Alcohol Services Now* mentioned that the brewers currently make only an insignificant contribution to the non-statutory alcoholism services. It was also noted that the Medical Council on Alcoholism received £25,000 from the Brewers' Society, and £10,000 from the Distillers to fund research. A contribution of £35,000 does not seem over-generous, in view of the size and wealth of the drinks industry.

As we have seen, there is a nationwide problem of drink abuse. The drink industry spends a great deal of money on advertising its products, and precious little on the prevention and amelioration of drinking problems. In this event, it is left to government to fill the breach. If, for the moment, we concentrate only on government advertising, an illuminating picture emerges. Bear in mind that six major brewers spent a total of £17.468 million on advertising their products in 1979. In the same year, the Health Education Council spent £17,600 on campaigns to publicize the dangers of alcohol abuse (Hansard 26 March 1980). Again, in 1979, the Ministry of Transport spent a total of £1,317,800 on the 'Don't Drink and Drive' campaign (Hansard 31 March 1980). The drinks industry spends very large sums of money on advertising in the expectation of making very much larger profits. The government spends relatively small amounts of money on advertising the dangers of alcohol abuse because, one might imagine, in purely financial terms, alcohol abuse costs the nation very little. Nothing could be further from the truth.

National cost of alcohol abuse

The true cost to the nation of alcohol abuse is unknown. There are many reasons for this state of affairs, not least important being the absence or incompleteness of much relevant data. An extensive range of factors is likely to contribute to the total cost, but it is important for the reader to gain some appreciation of the complexities involved. In this way, the problems inherent in arriving at a satisfactory estimate of the cost to the nation of alcohol abuse will become apparent. Consider the hypothetical case of a small private engineering concern that is being run by an owner/manager, with a work-force of nine. Let us imagine that the owner is responsible for managerial functions, such as seeking orders, negotiating prices, keeping up stocks of materials and negotiating their costs and future planning. We can sketch out what might happen if this businessman progressively increases his drinking to the point of experiencing severe drinking problems. The following scenario is anything but complete, and the reader might care to elaborate it or construct others as they might apply to other occupations.

Suppose our small industrialist has one or more hangovers every week. If he sometimes works 'at the bench', as many owners of small businesses do, his output may fall and he may waste materials. At the managerial level, his decision-making may be impaired and he may fail to obtain or may lose orders. If he has progressed to the point of being habitually affected by drink, the above problems are likely to exist, but more intensely and chronically. Furthermore, it is likely that our businessman will seek medical assistance for the effects of his excessive drinking. These effects may include anxiety, depression, sleeping difficulties, gastric problems, accidents, and so forth. Thus, it is at this point, if not earlier, that costs to the National Health Service (NHS) are involved. The point may next be reached where our man's personal functioning is severely affected by his alcohol abuse. All the above considerations apply but to an even greater extent. He may be so debilitated that his business collapses. His staff become unemployed and receive state unemployment benefit. The erstwhile businessman may, himself, receive unemployment or sickness benefit, while his family might gain extra support through Supplementary Benefit payments. It is very likely that there will be additional costs to the NHS while, at this stage or earlier, involvement in crime, traffic offences, or road accidents may occur. Involvement in crime will incur police and legal costs leading, maybe, to support for the individual, and his family, if he is imprisoned. If the crime is against property, there may be a cost to an insurance company. Road accidents may involve an even wider range of costs arising from the involvement of the police, fire service, NHS, the legal profession, insurance payments, and so forth. Finally, let us suppose that his excessive drinking leads this unhappy businessman to seek help from his general practitioner. If medication is prescribed there is an immediate cost to the NHS. Our alcohol abuser is likely to be referred to hospital or a unit that specializes in treating alcohol abusers. Such a unit might be an 'alcoholism unit' in a psychiatric hospital, or a non-statutory, voluntary agency. For example, many of the National Council on Alcoholism's 'Information Centres' provide counselling, and some run treatment programmes. Hopefully, it should now be clear that the financial cost to the nation of excessive drinking is difficult to determine and is multi-faceted. No financial equivalent can be estimated for misery experienced by the alcohol abuser and his or her family.

Some attempts have been made to estimate the financial cost to the nation of excessive drinking. In 1976, the Blennerhassett Committee produced a document for the Department of the Environment entitled: *Drinking and Driving*. The report suggested that the cost of road accidents due to drinking might be in the region of £100 million per annum. In 1979, the Royal College of Psychiatrists noted that admissions to NHS psychiatric hospitals in England and Wales for the treatment of alcoholism stood at about 13,500 per annum. They estimated the yearly cost of that hospital care to be in excess of £4 million. More recently, attempts have been made to obtain an estimate of the total financial cost to society of alcohol abuse. Holtermann and Burchell (1981) distinguished six factors that they claimed contribute to the social cost, and they provided both 'low' and 'high' estimates for each. Their main factor is loss of output, which they calculated to be between £331 and £538 million per annum. The cost to the NHS was given as £38 to £52 million. While acknowledging the tentative and incomplete nature of their estimates, they arrived at a total yearly social cost of £428 to £650 million resulting from alcohol abuse. In a later article, Maynard and Kennan (1981) discussed the Holtermann and Burchell estimates, emphasizing the many difficulties and imponderables involved. However, merely by updating the information used in the Holtermann and Burchell estimates, Maynard and Kennan arrived at a 1981 cost to society of £698.4 to £1,064.1 million. These are quite staggering sums of money by anyone's standards.

Clearly, any attempt to reduce the cost to society of alcohol abuse must aim at reducing the extent of alcohol abuse itself. Ways in which this might be accomplished will be discussed later, but there are several important barriers to such attempts. Currently, we have no means of assessing the broad social and economic benefits that accrue from the use of alcohol. Efforts to reduce alcohol abuse would have to stem from the political level, but judgements and decisions at that level may be influenced by a range of powerful and mutually conflicting interests (Office of Health Economics 1981). Prevarication and inactivity are most likely to prevail in the absence of firm data and research-based recommendations. For that very reason, substantial resources should be made available to obtain the information needed for rational decision-making by government. However, that same information should also be used to raise public awareness of the extent of the problem, and its costs, so that public pressure can be brought to bear on government to act.

Chapter 4

Personal, occupational and regional factors in relation to drinking and drinking problems

Age and the law

British law is relatively straightforward in the way it seeks to regulate alcohol consumption with respect to age. For example, intoxicating liquor must not be given to any child under the age of 5 years, except by order of a doctor and for some other good reason. Children under 14 years of age may not be in a bar during the 'permitted hours' (when intoxicants are on sale), although there are several provisos. Liqueur chocolates must not be sold to individuals under the age of 16 years, although a 16-year-old can buy beer, porter, cider or perry to drink with a meal that is being eaten in a part of a licensed premises (not the bar) that is set apart for dining. Having attained the age of 18 years, a person can legally buy and consume intoxicants on licensed premises.

Age, sex, drinking and drinking problems

There is a longstanding social expectation that different age groups will have different drinking habits. In practice, this expectation is largely fulfilled as a consequence of social and financial pressures. Until relatively recently, at least, young people simply lacked the money to buy liquor, as did the elderly. It follows that those with the money, the adult working population, were the largest consumers. Aside from purely financial considerations, there was a traditional general expectation that children would not drink alcohol, that the middle-aged would have moderate well-established drinking patterns, and that the elderly would be light, 'contemplative' drinkers. Thus, the middle-aged and elderly drinkers were expected to drink in a sociable manner. Less moderate, less stable drinking by young adults, those in their late teens and early twenties, was, and probably still is, regarded indulgently. After all, that is the period of life when mild behavioural excesses and experimentation provide the prelude to moderate, increasingly socialized, behaviour. Overall, social and financial factors have been heavily involved in shaping the stereotypes, outlined above. This is also true of the traditional differences between the sexes in their typical drinking patterns. Society expected and still expects women to drink more moderately than men. In particular, female heavy drinking and, worse still, drunkenness are regarded with strong disapproval by society at large. In contrast, there is the male stereotype that being able to hold his drink, is the infallible sign of a 'real' man. The reader will no doubt make the appropriate connections between these male and female stereotypes, and the fact that they originated in a strongly male-dominated society. Represented in their extreme forms, the male 'machismo' stereotype is one of a heavy habitual drinker who manages not to make a fool of himself or to fall on his face in a drunken stupor. In contrast, the female stereotype is of a light drinker who toys with alcohol and who unfailingly retains her ladylike composure. It is important to bear in mind that different expectations and stereotypes exist in different sections of society, the above stereotypes being chosen to highlight the male/female differences.

On the whole, the age-related drinking patterns revealed by a variety of community surveys do broadly support the traditional view. A survey conducted in the London borough of Camberwell, in the mid-1960s, showed that 55 per cent of 18- to 34-year-old males drank moderately or heavily, while only 30 per cent of those aged 50 years or more fell into the same drinking categories. In stark contrast, only 11 per cent of the younger age group women were moderate or heavy drinkers, with 2 per cent of the older age group having similar drinking levels. Hence, the younger age group drank more heavily than the older one, the males drinking more heavily than the females. A more recent survey of drinking in England and Wales was carried out by Wilson (1980a), on behalf of the Department of Health and Social Security (DHSS). Nearly 2,000 adults aged 18 or older were interviewed in their own homes, and asked about their drinking over the preceding seven days. Similar trends in drinking patterns were found to those reported in the Camberwell survey. The younger age groups drank more than the older, and men drank more than women. About 75 per cent of the men and 60 per cent of the women had consumed alcohol in the previous week. The average consumption for these drinkers was 20.3 units for the men (equivalent to about $1\frac{1}{2}$ pints of beer, or 3 singles of spirits each week day) and 7.2 units for the women (equivalent to about $\frac{1}{2}$ pint of beer or one single of spirits per day). Wilson noted that both sexes in the youngest (18–24 years) age group drank considerably more than those in the older age groups. Similar data are also available for Scotland and Northern Ireland (Wilson 1980b). Furthermore, using the criteria for 'safe' drinking proposed by the Royal College of Psychiatrists (1979), and having taken into account probable under-reporting by the heavier drinkers, Wilson (1980a) noted that the youngest age group contained the highest proportions of those who had exceeded the safe limits (13 per cent of the men, and 4 per cent of the women). The consistent trends are those of heavier drinking by the younger age groups, and by men.

So far in this discussion the data provided are 'cross-sectional' rather than 'longitudinal' in nature. In other words, the data are derived from a cross-section, or representative group, of people at one particular time. Age groups, and types of drinkers, are compared, but trends over time cannot be uncovered. However, it is the trends over time, the changes that may be occurring from year to year, that are of particular importance if we wish to know whether things are improving or deteriorating. Likewise, we must know about trends over time if we are to make worthwhile predictions about the future course of events.

It is an undisputed fact that the per capita consumption of alcohol has increased dramatically over the last two decades, at least (see Ch. 2). In a similar vein, there has been an increase in convictions for drunkenness in England and Wales, over the period 1968 to 1978, from 79,070 to 106,814 respectively. This is an increase of 35.1 per cent. The corresponding increase for men was 32.5 per cent, and for women 74.1 per cent. The relative increase for women was more than twice that for men. As reported in Chapter 1, during the period 1970–77, admissions to psychiatric hospitals and alcoholism units of individuals with primary diagnoses of alcoholism or alcoholic psychosis increased. Increases in female admissions were almost twice as high as for males but, significantly, the largest increases for both sexes was in the under 25-year-old groups. It is extremely unfortunate that national data concerning age and sex-related drinking do not exist over the last two or three decades. In consequence, it is not known how the increases in national consumption is distributed across age and sex groupings. It is not possible to provide direct evidence to answer the important question: 'Are the young drinking more than they used to?' Plausible inferences can be made on the basis of the indirect evidence provided above.

It is known that the consumption of alcohol has increased over the last two decades. Young people have become an increasingly powerful market force over the last three decades, at least, by virtue of their increased spending power. It is reasonable to expect this increased spending power to have been reflected, in part, in increased alcohol consumption. Admissions to treatment facilities for serious problem drinking have increased during the 1970s, particularly in the under 25-year-old age groups. The implication is that this group is drinking more heavily. Convictions for drunkenness have shown a mainly upward trend over the last two decades, convictions being proportionally higher in the 18- to 21-year-old group. The general rate of increase has been highest in the same group, since about 1966. This also suggests that it is this young group that has been increasing its alcohol consumption. Overall, there is no single, conclusive piece of evidence which demonstrates that young people are drinking more heavily than they were two decades ago, but it is difficult to provide more parsimonious explanations for the increased medical and legal drink-associated problems observed in that group. The weight of indirect evidence strongly supports the view that the young are drinking more and, as a result, some are experiencing adverse consequences.

Age, sex, social class, beverage and drinking venue

The recent survey by Wilson (1980a) of drinking in England and Wales showed that age and sex influence the type of beverage consumed, and the drinking venue. First, however, it is worth noting that 6 per cent of the men and 11 per cent of the women were abstainers, the proportion of non-drinkers increasing with age, for both sexes. Male drinkers are more likely to drink in pubs than are women. This is true of all age groups. More than half the male drinkers' drinking is likely to be carried out in bars, although the proportion declines from 78 per cent for the 18- to 24-year-old group to 52 per cent for the 55+ group. The reduction in bar drinking is compensated by a reciprocal rise in drinking at home. The pattern is more complex for women. The two male trends of reduced drinking in bars with advancing age and an increase in drinking at home were also found for women. The complicating fact is that only the youngest group was more likely to drink in bars (63 per cent), the remainder being more likely to drink at home. The most obvious explanation for this difference lies in the differing sex roles of men and women, a difference that is accentuated by the advent of children.

The sexes differ in the typical types of beverage they drink. Beer is by far the commonest drink for men, representing 87 per cent of all alcohol consumption by the youngest age group (18–24 years) and 66 per cent by the oldest (55+ years). This reduced proportion of beer drinking with age is balanced by an increase in spirit and wine drinking. The female pattern of beverage used is more complex and involves less variation, overall. Beer is marginally the most popular drink in the 18- to 24-year age group, representing 37 per cent of its total consumption. The decline in beer drinking with age is relatively slight, at 31 per cent in the oldest group. The outstanding difference between the sexes is the greater proportion of wine drinking by women. This is most pronounced in their choice of fortified wines (that is sherry, port or vermouth). Wines represented 48 per cent of the women's beverage consumption among the 25- to 34-year-olds, declining to 44 per cent in the oldest (55+) group.

The survey showed that, without exception, there were smaller proportions of heavy drinkers among married than amongst single, divorced and separated individuals. Single people of either sex were more likely to drink in bars than elsewhere, they were more likely to drink beer, and they drank more frequently each week. Heavier drinking among women was associated with being at work or being a full-time student, and having no dependent children. A likely explanation might be that childless working women have both more opportunities and more money to spend on drinking.

Social class, broadly defined by type of occupation, is

associated with different drinking venues and different types of beverages. Wilson (1980a) found that, for both men and women, manual workers were most likely to drink in bars. Non-manual male workers were more likely to drink in bars (53 per cent), whereas non-manual female workers were more likely to drink elsewhere (66 per cent). Typically, this meant drinking at home, either one's own home or someone else's. Beer, including lager, accounted for 84 per cent of the weekly consumption of the male manual workers, compared with 64 per cent for the non-manual sample. Interestingly, the consumption pattern of the latter group included equal proportions of wines and spirits. As before, the female pattern is more complex. Beer and wines represented the greatest proportion of beverages consumed by manual workers (37 per cent each), whilst wines were favoured by the non-manual group (54 per cent). In both groups the fortified wines represented the single most popular type of beverage (31 per cent for the non-manual, and 25 per cent for the manual).

The weekly pattern of drinking was also related to social class. In general terms, the non-manual workers spent more time drinking each week, but spread that drinking over more occasions. The average weekly consumption was a little higher for the manual workers of both sexes, the difference being marginal for females. Overall, the average consumption of alcohol per drinking occasion was higher for manual than non-manual workers, the difference being greatest for males.

In some respects, the drinking patterns described above correspond with the broad, British, drinking stereotypes relating age, sex, marital status and social class. It should be clear, though, that these stereotypes are crude, and conceal much subtle variation. For example, the youngest female group differs in some respects from the older age grouping, in a way that may owe something to the changing role of women in society. Again, the broad stereotypes do not take into account the influence of specific occupational and regional factors on drinking.

Occupational and regional influences associated with drinking and drinking problems

There is a wealth of anecdotal evidence and folklore suggesting that certain occupations are associated with heavy and frequent drinking, as well as unusually high occurrences of drink-associated problems. As is so often the case, some of the factors responsible for this state of affairs are obvious, whilst others are subtle and multiple. One would correctly anticipate that those whose occupations are directly concerned with producing or selling alcohol would drink more and experience more drinking problems. Publicans and barmen are, respectively, nine and five times more likely to die of liver cirrhosis than are men of comparable age (Registrar General 1957). Likewise, those working in the catering industry are also over-represented among heavy and problem drinkers. In Scotland, the distillery workers have had a tradition of 'draming' (sampling drams of the product) just as brewery workers have received a daily beer allowance as a perk of the job. Both groups are over-represented amongst heavy and problem drinkers.

Merchant seamen have traditionally been associated with heavy drinking and there is some evidence that they are at higher risk of developing drink-related problems. The exact reason for their heavier drinking is unclear but probably includes the fact that the dockside pub provided one comfortable and lively haven for them when in port during a voyage. Manual workers have tended to be heavy drinkers, partly, no doubt, because beer not only quenches the thirst but provides calories; steel workers and stokers, for example, sweat profusely and work up sizeable thirsts. Commercial travellers and business executives tend to be among the heavier drinkers, traditionally using alcohol, in part, to smooth the way for clinching deals with customers. Notice that in both occupations the cost of drinking is offset by the 'expense account'.

An incomplete list of occupations that tend to be associated with heavier alcohol consumption would include:

1. *Alcohol producers*: those working in the brewing, distilling and wine producing industries.
2. *Alcohol retailers and those whose work brings them into contact with alcohol*: publicans, bar and off-licence workers, hotel and restaurant serving staff, and caterers, etc.
3. *Those who lose a lot of water*: heavy manual workers, those working in hot atmospheres.
4. *Those who use alcohol in the course of their job to facilitate social interactions*: business executives, travelling salesmen, journalists, etc.
5. *Those whose jobs may involve high stress levels*: business executives, travelling salesmen, journalists, entertainers.
6. *Those whose jobs cause them to be away from home for extended periods*: seamen, travelling salesmen, itinerant construction workers, etc.
7. *Those whose occupation involves a strong drinking tradition*: printing trade workers, some building trades.
8. *Those whose occupation results in group cohesiveness that extends to social activities*: officers in the Armed Forces, etc.

No doubt combinations of these and other factors are active in promoting heavier than usual drinking among certain occupational groups.

Particular regions within countries have been shown to support differences in drinking habits. Once again, the survey by Wilson in England and Wales (1980a) provides some of the most recent data on this subject. The regions with the highest proportions of heavy drinkers were Wales, the North West and the North with 10.8, 10.5 and 9.8 per cent, respectively. It is unclear why this should be so, but it may be that the heavier drinking regions include more industrial workers. Those regions are associated with heavy industry, and the average disposable incomes have probably been higher in those same regions. These factors may partly account for their higher proportions of heavy drinkers.

Drawing upon a variety of sources, Wilson (1980a) provides further data on regional variations. The death rates from cirrhosis of the liver were highest in Greater London, followed by the North West, then the North. Lower death rates from the same cause were found in the East Midlands and, lowest of all, in East Anglia. Admissions to psychiatric hospitals, with a primary diagnosis of alcoholism or alcoholic psychosis, were proportionally highest in Greater London, the North West and the North, and the lowest in East Anglia and the East Midlands. Finally, convictions for drunkenness were highest in Greater London, the North West and the North, and lowest in the East Midlands and East Anglia. An important finding reported by Wilson was that there was a statistically significant association between the regional 'league tables' for the proportions of heavy drinkers and each of the corresponding regional league tables for drinking-problem rates (as indicated by mortality rates from cirrhosis of the liver, admissions for alcoholism or alcoholic psychosis, and convictions for drunkenness). This provides evidence that heavy drinking, and drink-related problems, go hand-in-hand. It does not indicate that the one always follows the other, only that the chances of it so doing are increased.

Before leaving the subject of regional variations, it is worthwhile emphasizing the complexities involved in interpreting, or 'making sense' of, the available data by briefly considering some statistics concerning England, Ireland, Scotland and Wales. Wilson (1980b) reported almost identical weekly average alcohol consumptions for English, Scottish and Welsh males, aged at least 20 years. The average Northern Irish male consumed at least one-quarter less than his other British counterparts. However, spirits account for 28 per cent of the weekly consumption among both Northern Irish and Scottish males, compared with 13 per cent for their English and Welsh counterparts. Going even beyond that, the drinking 'style' varies between areas. The Scottish male drinks on fewer occasions and spends less total time drinking than his English opposite number. The Northern Irish male drinks least often and for the least time. Conversely, the Northern Irish male drinks most per drinking occasion, and the English and Welsh least. Forty per cent of the Scottish men engaged in 'heavy' drinking on at least one day during the week prior to data collection, compared with 34 and 27 per cent of the Northern Irish, and English and Welsh, respectively. What this all amounts to is that the drinking style in Scotland tends to be more concentrated than in England and Wales; the Northern Irish occupying a middle position. The more concentrated Scottish drinking style would be expected to result in more frequent drunkenness than in the other three areas. Compared with the rest of the United Kingdom, a higher proportion of drinking in Northern Ireland took place in bars, while 31 per cent of the Northern Irish males, aged at least 20 years, were teetotal, in comparison with 6 and 7 per cent in England and Wales, and Scotland respectively. This indicates a more pronounced polarization of drinking behaviour in Northern Ireland than elsewhere in Great Britain. Thus, the Northern Irish male tends to be either a teetotaller, or someone who drinks relatively heavily in pubs mainly at the weekend.

Comparison of male and female drinking practices shows that, in broad detail, they are similar within the four areas of the United Kingdom. The main differences are that there were higher proportions of female than male teetotallers, and the women drank on fewer occasions, spent less total time drinking, drank less per occasion, drank more slowly, and did less of their drinking in bars. Furthermore, a smaller proportion of their weekly consumption comprised beer, with spirits, table wine and fortified wine representing a larger proportion. Interestingly, in Scotland and Northern Ireland, 49 and 58 per cent of the women's weekly consumption was spirits, the corresponding figures for their male counterparts being 28 per cent, in both cases.

The emerging picture is complex and its interpretation is difficult. We see that several factors, or variables, must be taken into account when attempting to characterize drinking practices. Similarly, except in some special cases, multiple explanations are necessary when attempting to account for the prevalence of drink-associated problems.

Chapter 5

The physical effects of alcohol

Absorption and metabolism

When one drinks alcohol, it is absorbed through the stomach walls and the intestines. The 'stronger' the drink – the higher its alcohol content up to about 40 per cent – the faster it is absorbed. Sweet drinks, those containing sugar, are absorbed more slowly than those containing no sugar. Conversely, the absorption of alcohol is accelerated in the case of carbonated drinks, those containing dissolved carbon dioxide gas. The rate at which alcohol is absorbed is affected by the stomach contents. Food can slow the absorbtion rate by up to 50 per cent. For a given intake, the faster the alcohol is absorbed, the higher the maximum alcohol concentration attained in the blood. Thus, as a given amount of alcohol is quickly absorbed, it will result in a higher maximum blood alcohol concentration than if the same amount of alcohol had been absorbed more slowly. As we shall see below, the higher the blood alcohol level the greater the physiological and psychological effects on the individual. In plain words, the higher the blood alcohol concentration, the greater the likelihood of intoxication, unconsciousness, coma and death, in that order. The age-old advice not to drink on an empty stomach is based on sound reasons; food slows the absorption of alcohol so that it is dealt with more easily by the metabolic processes. The consequences are that the blood alcohol level is less likely to rise steeply, so the individual is not incapacitated. It is worth noting, in passing, that about 2–5 per cent of the absorbed alcohol is eliminated unchanged through the lungs and kidneys. Moreover, the concentrations of alcohol in the expelled breath and in the urine are closely related to the blood and tissue alcohol levels. Hence, in cases of suspected drunken driving, the police may require the driver to perform the breathalyser test or provide urine or blood samples.

It is an important fact that alcohol does not need to be digested in order to be absorbed. It is able to pass directly via the stomach and intestinal walls into the bloodstream. However, the rate at which alcohol is metabolized depends upon a number of factors. For instance, a large intake of alcohol results in an increased rate of metabolism. Heavy drinkers are able to metabolize alcohol faster than light drinkers. Once the alcohol has been absorbed, it must be metabolized if its concentration in the bodily tissue is to fall and, eventually, return to zero. There is no other way currently available of eliminating absorbed alcohol from the body than via the natural process of metabolism. Large quantities of black coffee may enliven the individual through the action of the stimulant caffeine, but this does not eliminate the alcohol. Thus, the drunk who follows alcohol with plenty of strong black coffee, is likely to remain awake rather than to fall asleep. As a rough guide, it can be taken that the average-sized, average drinker will metabolize four pints of beer, or their equivalent, in about four to five hours. Twice the quantity of alcohol would require approximately twice the time (Royal College of Psychiatrists 1979).

Effects on bodily organs

When alcohol is drunk, its vapour enters the nasal cavities and the liquid bathes the taste buds. Even at low concentrations of alcohol the drinker's abilities to differentiate between odours and between tastes are impaired. At high concentrations, these effects are more severe. That is why unscrupulous bar workers are unlikely to be detected by average drinkers to whom they initially serve a high quality brand of spirits, only to follow that with an inferior brand. By the time the superior quality beverage has been drunk, the average drinker's ability to discriminate good from indifferent spirit has been impaired. Professional spirit blenders and tasters are exceptions to this general rule, of course.

Stomach

Having reached the stomach, the effects of alcohol depend upon a variety of factors. Small quantities of dilute alcohol increase the rate of digestive juice secretion from the stomach wall. In consequence, appetite is increased, whilst digestion is improved. This is why 'aperitifs' can perform a useful function. At alcohol concentrations of 40 per cent, or more, the stomach lining is irritated and inflamed, so that appetite is suppressed. Large quantities of alcohol can so irritate the stomach lining that involuntary expulsion (vomiting) of the stomach contents results. The fact that alcohol is a stomach irritant explains why those suffering the torments of gastric ulcers should abstain. Continual heavy drinking can result in the unpleasant stomach condition of gastritis, which manifests itself as severe 'indigestion'. In such cases, the gastritis may be chronic or ever present. It is estimated that in excess of 20 per cent of alcoholics develop peptic ulcers, that is stomach and duodenal ulcers (Royal College of Psychiatrists 1979). 'Burst' or 'perforated' peptic ulcers are a serious matter that can, if not treated promptly, result in death. Thus, alcoholics have a higher death rate from peptic and oesophageal ulcers than does the remainder of the population.

It was noted, above, that because of its relatively high calorific value (7.1 calories per gramme) alcohol can virtually replace normal food intake. If normal amounts of food are still eaten, despite a high alcohol intake, the result is likely to be an increase in body weight and, ultimately, obesity. The latter carries an increased mortality risk, hence life insurance premiums are higher for obese than for individuals of normal weight. If normal amounts of food are not eaten by the heavy drinker, body weight may remain normal, but vitamin and mineral deficiencies will probably occur. Eventually, the absence of a balanced diet can give rise to highly undesirable conditions such as scurvy, beri-beri, anaemia and poly-neuropathy. Equally, in the long run, malnutrition can so undermine an individual's constitution that vulnerability to a host of illnesses is increased. In everyday language, the individual's resistance to disease is undermined. Tuberculosis and pneumonia used to be major killers of alcoholics.

Cardiovascular system

From the stomach and intestines, alcohol passes into the blood stream. One immediate effect is to cause the tiny blood vessels in the skin (the cutaneous blood vessels) to dilate. This imparts a flushed appearance to the face that is accompanied by a feeling of warmth, and increased sweating. As the sweat evaporates it cools the skin which, under some circumstances, may cause a reduction in body temperature. That is why it is unwise to drink alcohol 'to warm oneself up' if the body is thoroughly chilled. The cutaneous blood vessels would dilate, warm blood would be drawn from deep within the body where a stable temperature is vital, and that blood would lose valuable heat through the skin. Ultimately, this could lead to a fatal loss of heat from the internal organs. For these reasons, exposure (hypothermia) victims should never be given alcohol in the hope of increasing their body temperature. Leaving aside the special case of hypothermia, large quantities of alcohol depress the body's temperature regulation. This can result in a large temperature reduction. Alcohol has no effect on the arteries.

Alcohol affects the action of the heart and, in extreme cases, the very substance of the heart. Moderate alcohol intake causes a small brief increase in heart rate. Concurrently, there is an increase in blood pressure. There is statistical evidence that alcoholism is associated with many forms of cardiovascular disease (Adelstein and White 1976). Cardiomyopathy results from the heart muscle becoming infiltrated by fat deposits. In plain language, the heart becomes fatty; a condition sometimes referred to as 'beer drinker's heart'. Fatty muscles are less powerful and less efficient than lean ones. Since the heart can be regarded as a muscular pump, it follows that a fat heart is less capable of pumping blood round the body. Alcoholic cardiomyopathy is directly attributable to a long-term, high alcohol intake. As with all heart diseases, cardiomyopathy is a serious matter. On the bright side, it is possible that the moderate use of alcohol may somewhat reduce the risk of coronary heart disease (Willett *et al.* 1980).

Kidneys

It is well known that drinking results in an increased urine production. This is not solely a matter of volumetric compensation. True, part of the increase in urine production does arise directly from the water content of all alcoholic beverages. However, there is also a more subtle mechanism at work. The pituitary gland is a small, ovoid structure that is attached to the base of the brain. Despite its small size (it weighs less than 1 g in an adult) it is the most important endocrine, or ductless, gland, since it has many functions. The action of alcohol on the pituitary gland depends upon whether the blood alcohol level is rising, falling or stable. If it is rising, urine production increases: if constant or falling, urine production is reduced and fluid is retained in the tissues.

Chronic excessive alcohol intake can give rise to the wasting, or degeneration, of major muscle groups. As a result of this process, large amounts of breakdown products are released into the bloodstream and are thereby transported to the kidneys for removal and ultimate expulsion from the body. The Royal College of Psychiatrists (1979) has suggested that, as a result of the above process, the kidneys may be subjected to an overload of such proportions that they fail, and death ensues. Apparently, this is a very rare occurrence.

Pancreas

The pancreas has the dual roles of manufacturing about 1 litre of digestive juice per day and of producing insulin and glucagon. Acute pancreatitis arises when the pancreas is attacked by the digestive enzymes that it produces. In effect, the pancreas begins to digest itself. This is a serious and painful disease that results in more or less immediate death for about one-tenth of its victims. Benjamin, Imrie and Blumgart (1977) have estimated that, of the 600 or so deaths in England from acute pancreatitis, perhaps one-quarter of them are associated with excessive drinking. It is clear that acute alcoholic pancreatitis occurs most frequently among young males. It will be recalled that this section of the population has the heaviest drinking patterns. A chronic form of pancreatitis also exists which may grumble along, or flare up from time to time.

Liver

Most readers will be aware that habitual heavy drinking can eventually damage the liver. There are various types of damage, but the most frequently associated with drinking is 'cirrhosis' of the liver. The word 'cirrhosis' is derived from a Greek word meaning 'tan-coloured'. This refers to the appearance of the cirrhosed liver. In cirrhosis, the normal cells die, to be replaced by fibrous scar tissue. The cirrhosed liver comprises tan-coloured islands of healthy liver cells, surrounded and separated by the scar tissue. Death from liver cirrhosis occurs when the liver is so badly affected that it is unable to fulfil its normal functions. The latter include the metabolism of nutrients, the neutralization of some hormones, the breakdown of drugs, the production of certain biochemicals that are necessary in maintaining normal blood circulation, and the extraction of toxic breakdown products from the blood.

Unfortunately, there are only the crudest of guidelines available to predict who is and who is not at risk of developing cirrhosis. The Royal College of Psychiatrists (1979) is clear that extreme chronic drinking, averaging more than 10 pints ($5\frac{1}{2}$ litres) of beer daily over 15 years, carries with it a 'grave risk' of liver damage. The Report goes on to point out that possibly 80 per cent of such drinkers will sustain liver damage. What, then, is a safe level for regular drinking? The same Report mentions evidence indicating an increased risk of cirrhosis arising from a regular intake equivalent to between 5 and 10 pints ($3-5\frac{1}{2}$ litres) of beer, or more, per day. Thus, the 'safe' maximum regular intake of alcohol that carries no increased risk of liver damage is probably lower than was previously thought to be the case.

It should be mentioned that drinking is not the only cause of cirrhosis, just as not all alcoholics develop liver cirrhosis. Only about two-thirds of alcoholics show evidence of liver damage, and only about one-tenth have cirrhosis. Other types of damage include fatty infiltration and alcoholic hepatitis. Also important, in Britain, over the last two decades alcohol-related cirrhosis has been accounting for a progressively larger proportion of all death from cirrhosis. Saunders *et al.* (1981) carried out a 20-year prospective study in the West Birmingham Health Area, covering the late 1950s to mid 1970s. Over that period, the incidence of cirrhosis tripled, while the proportion of alcohol-related cases rose from one- to two-thirds. In the mid 1970s, over 60 per cent of those with alcohol-related cirrhosis died within 5 years of their cirrhosis being diagnosed; a heavy toll, by any standards.

There is a sex difference in the incidence of alcohol-related liver cirrhosis. Donnan and Haskey (1977) reported the discharge and death rates associated with liver cirrhosis from non-psychiatric NHS hospitals in England and Wales over the period 1964–73. The male rates were higher than the female ones, when comparing similar age groups. Significantly, from our viewpoint, although the rates for non-alcohol-related cirrhosis were pretty well constant, the rates for alcohol-related cirrhosis increased in all age groups for both sexes. Donnan and Haskey provided data, from 1916–75, on the proportion of all deaths from cirrhosis of the liver that was attributable to alcoholic cirrhosis. Leaving aside the rather complex picture in the first half of the century, there have been sharp increases in the proportions of such deaths in both sexes, and it is the 15- to 34-year-old age group that shows the most pronounced change.

There is now good reason to believe that women are more susceptible to such damage than are men. Saunders *et al.* (1981) reviewed several survey reports, concluding that women develop liver damage in response to smaller quantities of alcohol over shorter periods of time. These authors suggested that it might be prudent to assume the 'safe' level of alcohol consumption for women to be half that for men.

Quite apart from the involvement of alcohol in some cases of liver cirrhosis and hepatitis, alcoholics have an increased risk of developing liver cancer (Royal College of Psychiatrists 1979); and on the subject of cancer, several studies have shown that heavier drinkers are at greater risk of developing cancers of the tongue, mouth, pharynx, larynx and oesophagus.

One final matter must be considered before leaving the subject of alcohol-induced liver damage, and that is the extent to which alcohol consumption and cirrhosis are related at national and international levels. Although this subject has been much debated in recent years, a consensus does seem to have developed. There is general agreement that the extent of alcohol-related problems in a country is related to the total, or mean per capita, alcohol consumption in that country. At its simplest: the higher the total or average consumption, the greater the number of alcohol-related problems, including liver cirrhosis. Table 5, which is based on data in the report by the Special Committee of the Royal College of Psychiatrists (1979), illustrates this relationship.

It can be seen that, overall, the three indices of 'damage' increase in line with the increase in alcohol consumption. When all the annual figures from 1950–75 are taken into account, the association between alcohol consumption and the three indices is not perfect but, in each case, it is statistically highly significant. International data for alcohol consumption and liver cirrhosis death rates reveal the same highly significant association. The data in Table 5 were taken from Popham, *et al.* (1975).

Table 5

Country	Per capita consumption in litres of absolute alcohol	Death from liver cirrhosis per 100,000 people over 20 years
France	24.66	51.7
Italy	18.00	30.5
Portugal	17.57	48.0
West Germany	13.63	29.0
Belgium	8.42	14.2
UK	7.66	4.1
Denmark	7.50	11.6
Finland	4.16	5.4

The table reveals one anomalous result, that of Denmark. The British and Danish alcohol consumption are very similar, but the Danish death rate from liver cirrhosis is almost three times greater than that of the UK. Likewise, the Italian and Portuguese consumption figures were 18.00 and 17.57 respectively. Yet the corresponding death rates were 30.5 and 48.0. The general rule, that the greater the national consumption the higher the liver cirrhosis death rate, clearly holds but some data do not fit into such a simple picture. Indeed, there is no doubt that many factors influence the relation between alcohol consumption and associated damage, both at national and international levels. It may be that the continual heavy consumption which characterizes French drinking may conspire to produce high cirrhosis rates. In contrast, intermittent heavy binge drinking may give rise to higher rates of drink-related legal offending rather than cirrhosis (Smith 1981a).

Brain and nervous system

The transient (acute) effects of alcohol on the brain and nervous system will be given detailed consideration in the next chapter. Here, we shall review some of the long-term (chronic) effects. Long-term, very heavy drinking may result in damage to the central and peripheral nervous systems. The former comprises the brain and spinal cord, the latter the nerves that radiate from the spinal cord. We shall briefly consider some of the neurological disorders that can result from long-term excessive drinking, but it should be noted that several such disorders may be present by the time the drinker seeks medical help.

Peripheral neuropathy is a condition affecting about 10 per cent of chronic alcoholics (Victor 1975). It refers to the degeneration and break down of the peripheral nerves. Either the legs alone or, less commonly (30 per cent of cases), the legs and arms are involved. The symptoms include weakness, pain, tenderness of the muscles and, often, the 'burning feet' syndrome. Typically, the symptoms first appear in the feet, progressing up the legs and, in some cases, to the arms. The symptoms are usually present on both sides of the body, and they are debilitating. The exact cause of the condition is uncertain, except that it is due to some nutritional deficiency. Nutritional neuropathy is well documented and occurs in many guises, such as beri beri and pellagra. Alcoholics whose

Table 6 The relationship between alcohol consumption, drunkenness convictions, cirrhosis deaths and hospital admissions in the UK

Year	Average per capita alcohol consumption in litres of 100% alcohol	Drunkenness convictions per 10,000 of the population	Cirrhosis deaths per million of the population	Hospital admissions with primary diagnosis of alcoholism or alcoholic psychosis
1950	5.2	14.0	23	1,053
1955	5.3	15.8	26	2,479
1960	5.8	19.3	28	5,774
1965	6.5	19.8	29	8,091
1970	7.3	21.6	28	12,751
1975	9.4	27.0	37	

diet is well balanced do not experience peripheral neuropathy. Currently, it is believed that the condition results from the concurrent deficiency of many vitamins, although the B-complex, in particular, appears to be heavily implicated. Treatment involves an adequate diet and dosing with multi-vitamins. Improvements occur slowly because the nerves have to regenerate. After one or two years of treatment, recovery is usually as far advanced as it will ever be, but it may never be complete.

In a small percentage of alcoholics the part of the brain known as the cerebellum is affected, giving rise to the cerebellar syndrome. The most visible symptom is that of locomotor ataxia, in which the co-ordination required when walking is impaired. The individual walks with difficulty, using short hurried steps. The foot is lifted well clear of the ground, but the leg is thrown forward, so that the heel descends forcibly. There is often a pronounced reduction in the senses of touch and pain. Sometimes the cerebellar syndrome involves the upper limbs. In such cases co-ordination is again affected, making it difficult or impossible to grasp and manipulate small objects. Picking up things, buttoning clothing and even feeding oneself becomes problematic.

Of the several remaining neurological disorders that can arise from long-term excessive drinking, yet to be mentioned here will be the Wernicke–Korsakoff Syndrome. In fact, Wernicke's encephalopathy and Korsakoff's psychosis are different facets of the same disease. The usual course of the syndrome starts with Wernicke's encephalopathy, in which the patient is confused, may exhibit a variety of eye and motor paralyses, as well as ataxia. If this condition is acute and untreated, the individual may die. Since Wernicke's encephalopathy is caused by thiamine (Vitamin B_1) deficiency, treatment involves dosing the patient with that vitamin. Recovery may be complete within a few days or weeks. In more than three-quarters of these cases the patient recovers, only to manifest Korsakoff's syndrome.

This is a chronic amnesic condition in which recent memories are lost and new memories are not established. Memories from the distant past are usually fully intact. Additional symptoms include a loss of initiative and, in some cases, confabulation. The latter refers to the fabrication by means of which the individual attempts to present a coherent, rather than a fragmented, account of the recent past. Curiously, the patient fails to recognize the intellectual deficit that assails him. Korsakoff's syndrome is sometimes preceded by Wernicke's encephalopathy; it most frequently occurs after an attack of delirium tremens (see the next chapter). Treatment usually involves the administration of multi-vitamins, and custodial care is often necessary. The prognosis, or outlook, for the individual with Korsakoff's syndrome is typically poor. The condition usually persists, to a greater or lesser extent.

Foetal alcohol syndrome

When a pregnant woman drinks alcohol, it can pass from her bloodstream through the placenta, and into the bloodstream of her unborn child. There is evidence that heavy drinking can cause damage to the foetus, including an unusually small head, congenital orthopaedic and cardiac disorders, cleft palate, and some degree of mental handicap. This collection of symptoms, some or all of which may be present in afflicted infants, is known as the 'foetal alcohol syndrome'. As with many of the disorders referred to in this chapter, the precise mechanisms that cause the syndrome and, in particular, the part played by alcohol, all remain unclear. The prevalence of the syndrome is currently unknown but studies now underway in the USA should provide some of the answers to these important questions. The most immediately important information for pregnant drinkers would be some indication of the 'safe' drinking limit. The Report of the Royal College of Psychiatrists acknowledges the lack of definitive information on this point, but suggests that a daily alcohol consumption equivalent of two bottles of wine may well put the foetus at risk. Given the gravity of the foetal alcohol syndrome, mothers-to-be may feel it wise to drink much more moderately than this.

Mortality

There is no doubt that a significant association exists between excessive drinking and an increased risk of death, or mortality rate. Excessive drinkers are likely to die at an earlier age than their moderate-drinking fellows. Adelstein and White (1976) examined the official records of 2,070 alcoholics who had been admitted to, or discharged from, psychiatric hospitals in England and Wales during or before 1964. By July 1974, 794 (38.4 per cent) of them had died. The comparable figure for the population at large, taking age into consideration, is 358.8. Overall, the death rate for alcoholics was over twice (2.2) that of the general population. This difference is present in all age groups, but is inversely related to age. Thus, alcoholics in the age range 15–39 years have a death rate of nearly twelve times that of similarly aged people in the population at large. The figures for the 40–59 and 60+ age ranges are 3.6 and 1.4 respectively. The youngest age group is most at risk. For reasons that are unclear, female alcoholics have relatively higher mortality rates than their male counterparts of similar age. The most striking example is in the youngest (15–39 years) age group. In that case, females have a death rate 17.4 times higher than in the general population of the same age, compared to an 11.5 ratio for males. The reasons for this sex difference in mortality ratios are unknown and, consequently, open to speculation. Adelstein and White (1976) noted that excessive drinking is less prevalent in females than in males, and that the number of female alcoholics is 'considerably smaller' than the number of male alcoholics. These authors speculate that, in view of these facts, female alcoholics may be socially and behaviourally more dissimilar from the average female, than male alcoholics are from their average, non-alcoholic peers. This notion that female alcoholics are more 'deviant' from the population at large than are their male counterparts is not new. However, it could be that females are inherently more vulnerable than males to the effects of excessive drinking. Evidence consistent with the latter view comes from a recent review by Saunders *et al.* (1981) of sex differences in the incidence of alcoholic liver disease. They concluded that liver disease tends to be more severe in women when they first seek help. This could be due to a number of social facts. However, these authors also found that these women presented themselves for treatment after a shorter period of excessive drinking, having had a lower daily alcohol consumption than their male peers. This is consistent with the speculation that women are more vulnerable than men to alcoholic liver disease. If this higher vulnerability does exist, it may do so for a range of alcohol-related physical damage and, in consequence, be one factor that results in the higher female mortality ratios. Saunders *et al.* suggested that the 'safe' regular daily alcohol consumption for women should be regarded as being half that for men: no more than 40 g alcohol against 80 g respectively.

Alcohol and other drugs

Alcohol may interact with other drugs that the drinker is taking. When physicians prescribe drugs, they sometimes advise against drinking alcohol whilst the prescribed drug is in the body. A failure to heed this advice may have unpleasant, dangerous, or in the extreme case, fatal consequences. The combination of some sleep-inducing drugs and alcohol may result in coma, followed by death. The effects of minor tranquillizers may be greatly enhanced when alcohol is consumed, while drugs that interfere with the metabolism of alcohol may give rise to nausea, vomiting, headache and falling blood pressure, as a consequence of acetaldehyde build up (Royal College of Psychiatrists 1979). Alcohol should not be consumed by people taking antidepressants, or who are taking certain powerful pain-relieving drugs. This by no means exhausts the list of dangerous alcohol/drug combinations. Hopefully, it may serve to emphasize the necessity of heeding medical advice not to drink when taking certain medicines.

Having reviewed some of the physical effects of alcohol, let us now turn to the psychological effects.

Chapter 6

Psychological effects of drinking

Alcohol is consumed because of its effects on the brain and nervous system. (One commercial consequence of this is that non-alcoholic 'beers' and 'wines' are unlikely ever to replace their conventional, alcohol-containing counterparts.) Pharmacologically, alcohol is a central nervous system depressant. This is counter-intuitive because, at blood alcohol levels associated with pronounced intoxication, alcohol seems to act as a stimulant. Alcohol tends to make the drinker more sociable, lively, easily amused, relaxed, talkative, self-accepting, and self-assured, for example. How, then, can it be a depressant? This is best understood in terms of factors within as well as outside the individual. Within the individual, the brain contains many inhibitory circuits. The important point is that the activity of any one part may be moderated by one or more inhibitory circuits or mechanisms. A mechanical analogy would be the regulation of an engine's speed by means of a governor, whilst an electronic analogy would be in terms of 'negative feedback' circuitry. Were the governor to be removed from the engine, the latter would probably run beyond its safe limit and damage itself. If the negative feedback circuitry were removed from the electronic apparatus, electrical distortion, overloading and subsequent damage would probably occur. In the case of the human brain, reducing the 'strength' or 'power' of the inhibitory circuits would result in an increase in activity of the areas that those circuits normally modify. The quiet person who usually speaks only when spoken to may become lively and talkative. The shy individual may become sociable, and the meek may become argumentative. The apparent stimulating effect of alcohol results when the inhibitory processes in the brain are depressed, or 'damped down'. The process is one of 'disinhibition'.

Having outlined the mechanism by which alcohol produces its widely valued 'stimulating' effect, an important proviso must be added. Alcohol produces disinhibition in the brain, but it does not determine the type of behaviour that results. This is a function of some admixture of the individual's culture, immediate environment, experience, expectations, mood before drinking, and so forth. That is why the sad person may become utterly miserable or elated, as a result of drinking. That is also why some people seem unaffected by drink until they collapse in a heap. Up to a certain point, alcohol does not determine the nature of the psychological changes that occur, but it does act as a catalyst for those changes. Beyond that 'certain point', the general depressant effect on brain activity leads to a 'damping down' of motor behaviour, intellectual (or 'cognitive') processing and emotions. Ultimately, at high enough blood alcohol concentrations the activity of the brain is reduced to such an extent that unconsciousness, followed by coma and finally death, may result. One final word of caution. In referring to a 'certain point', above, it should not be taken that there is a specific point at which the apparent stimulating effects of drinking suddenly change to a depressant effect. Some functions may appear to be stimulated at the same time that others are depressed. The change-over is not sudden but progressive. Likewise, although the psychological effects of drinking described in this chapter are separated into the behavioural, cognitive (intellectual) and affective (emotional) areas, the effects of a particular blood alcohol level may be more or less pronounced in each area. Alcohol affects the whole person in all areas of functioning.

Drinking and behaviour

For a particular blood alcohol concentration, the more complex the behaviour required of the drinker the more detrimental the effects of that alcohol on performance. Reaction time, the length of time taken to respond to a signal (stimulus), is increased at blood levels in excess of 50 mg per cent. The degree of impairment is greatest with tests requiring speed and a sustained performance in response to complex stimuli. As noted in the Report of the Special Committee, this finding has important implications for drinking and driving (Royal College of Psychiatrists 1979). At a blood alcohol concentration of 80 mg per cent, the legal limit in the UK, driving is 'seriously' affected. It has been estimated that about two-thirds of all drivers killed at night have blood alcohol levels in excess of 80 mg per cent (Department of the Environment 1976). At a blood alcohol level of around 100 mg per cent, the individual is appreciably more impulsive and likely to take risks and at the same time showing impaired co-ordination, or clumsiness, and drowsiness. Blood alcohol levels of 150 mg are associated with very severe motor and sensory deficits, including gross unsteadiness when standing and walking, disturbed balance, gross speech defects, double vision, extreme sleepiness. Stupor, anaesthesia, in fact extreme intoxication, are displayed by the vast majority of drinkers at about 300 mg per cent. Coma occurs at around 500 mg per cent, and death supervenes in the region of 500–800 mg per cent. The reader might be wondering whether tolerance for alcohol alters the behavioural consequences of the above blood alcohol concentrations. Most of us know or have known individuals who can really 'hold their drink' and 'drink most people under the table'. The evidence of our own eyes suggests that such drinkers are exceptions to the general rule. Experimental studies have shown that, to a limited extent, this is so. However, this is an instance in which appearance does not faithfully reflect reality. Nobody who drinks is immune from the pharmacological effects of alcohol. Some alcohol-tolerant drinkers demonstrate *less* impairment on *some* tasks; but that is all. In the case of driving, the mere ability of a drinker to walk to the car does not guarantee that he or she is in a fit state to drive. That is one reason for police dissatisfaction with the old test of getting suspected drunken drivers to 'walk the line'. Too many obviously drunken drivers demonstrated an unexpected ability to perform that (simple) behavioural task without difficulty.

When considering the subject of alcohol-associated accidents, driving accidents are but one type. It is probably less well recognized that alcohol is known to be implicated in death due to accidental fires. Likewise, several surveys of head-injured patients have found that large proportions of those patients had alcohol in their blood when the accident happened. In their prospective study of over 2,000 diagnosed alcoholics, Adelstein and White (1976) found higher rates of accidents, poisoning and violence in all age groups, than would be expected among people of similar age in the general population. When all age groups were combined, the male alcoholics were twenty-four times more likely to suffer from these misfortunes, and female alcoholics nearly eighteen times more likely to do so. Physicians have long known that it is wise to enquire about the drinking habits of patients who repeatedly consult because of broken bones, especially ribs, cuts and bruises.

It is a general observation that heavy drinkers, not least of all alcoholics, are fairly often 'polydrug' users; that is to say, they use and abuse a variety of drugs, prescribed and unprescribed. (Attend a gathering of alcoholics at an open meeting of Alcoholics Anonymous, for example, and the air soon becomes almost unbreathable due to tobacco smoke.) Apart from heavy drinkers often being heavy smokers and copious drinkers of strong tea or coffee, they may also become reliant upon drugs to calm their fraught nerves, and to get them to sleep. While it is difficult enough to moderate or desist from harmful drinking, poly- or multiple-drug users are confronted by a more difficult problem still.

There is good reason to believe that sexually deviant acts, such as sexual assaults on women and children, when perpetrated by normally upright citizens, are quite often carried out while intoxicated. These appear to be instances in which, due to the disinhibiting effects of alcohol, sexual fantasies are acted upon in the real world. When sobered up, the typical response of the perpetrator is one of disbelief, horror and shame.

It has long been known that there is an association between alcohol and crime. Numerous studies have shown that prison populations have a higher incidence of drinking problems than is found in a matched group of non-offenders. Studies in England and Scotland have indicated that in excess of half the male and about 15 per cent of the female prisoners have 'serious' drinking problems (Royal College of Psychiatrists 1979). The majority of these offenders are guilty of petty offences: not of important or serious crimes. They are usually only marginally integrated into society, existing on the fringe. Their offences are often impulsive and, when carried out under the influence of alcohol, farcically inept. Many such petty offenders are in and out of prison for a large part of their lives, having no conventional occupational skills, no social ties, and no way of escaping from the downward spiral. Ultimately, petty recidivism becomes a way of life. One of the few satisfactions available to those living in this way may be drinking which, under the circumstances, is likely to keep them locked into their way of life.

At the other end of the same spectrum are those prisoners who have carried out serious crimes whilst intoxicated. These include hit-and-run drivers, arsonists, those who have been found guilty of inflicting severe physical injury on others and, at the extreme, murder. These offenders are on the 'same spectrum' in that their crimes were carried out impulsively, when their habitual inhibitions against extreme behaviour of this sort were lifted by alcohol. There is evidence from several countries that a large proportion of those convicted of murder and other violent crimes had been drinking prior to the offence (Evans 1980).

At a different level are those 'professional' criminals who develop drinking problems. One can envisage many ways in which their very occupation may lead them to drink excessively. Meetings between criminals may routinely be conducted in pubs and clubs; two traditional meeting places for members of the underworld. Since the immediate period before a crime is likely to be tense, some offenders may develop a reliance upon alcohol to stiffen their resolve. Traditional working-class recreations such as drinking and gambling may be indulged in more frequently given the lump sum of money from the last 'job'. The sudden availability of a large sum of money may encourage heavier drinking than would be possible to a weekly wage earner.

Mention has already been made, above, of an association between alcohol and violence, but it is worthwhile considering this finding in a little more detail to avoid gaining the impression that the linkage is straightforward. The association between alcohol and violence is put into perspective when it is remembered that alcohol is usually involved in only a minority of the violent incidents that are reported. Under these circumstances, alcohol cannot be more than one of several causes of violence. It has been suggested that alcohol may increase 'aggression' in human beings by raising the level of the male hormone, testosterone. The presence of sufficiently high levels of the latter appear to be necessary if a variety of animal species are to display aggressive behaviours. Unfortunately, alcohol is known to depress testosterone levels, while direct attempts to relate testosterone levels to aggressive behaviour and to self-reported hostility have been unsuccessful. The association between rape and alcohol provides a good example of the complexity of that association. There is a high incidence of alcoholism among convicted rapists, and various studies have reported that, on average, 40 per cent of rapists have been drinking before committing rape. These findings can be explained in a large number of ways without recourse to any notion that alcohol was the primary cause of the offence. The fact that alcohol depresses the critical faculties and impairs judgement in itself provides the basis for an 'explanation'. The rapist may grossly misinterpret the wishes and willingness of his victim-to-be, so that what was never intended to be a rape, becomes just that. Again, the intention to commit rape may have been there all along, alcohol simply providing the resolve to go ahead. Given that investigators obtain their information from convicted rapists, it is possible that these offenders exaggerate the extent of their drinking before the rape in order to excuse their behaviour. Some may believe that blaming alcohol may cause a court to take a more lenient view of their crime and, thus, impose a lighter sentence. Notice too that these informants are rapists who have been caught and convicted. It is well established that only a minority of rape victims report their assault to the police. Some estimates suggest that only one-tenth of all rapes are reported. Under such circumstances there is no way of knowing what proportion of unreported rapes are associated with drinking. It also appears that in many cases not only the rapist but the victim had been drinking prior to the offence. It will be clear to the reader that no simple statement can be made about the nature of the association between alcohol and rape. Similar difficulties also arise in relation to the association between alcohol and child abuse, violence towards spouses, accidental injury and suicide. In the latter case, alcoholics are known to be over-represented in the suicide statistics, while several studies have shown that successful suicide victims drank alcohol shortly before their deaths. It is safe to guess that there is no single, simple causal connection between drinking and the suicidal behaviour.

In general terms, human behaviour is complexly determined, so simple explanations could hardly be valid.

Drinking and cognition

That alcohol affects cognitions, or intellectual functions, is recognized by drinkers and abstainers alike. The drinker who has had 'too much' to drink may be more confiding, frank and outspoken about 'sensitive' matters than when completely sober. Likewise, such an individual may be more flirtatious, more boisterous, and less socially adept than he or she would be not having consumed alcohol. All these behaviours indicate a change in the criteria, or a change in attitude towards the criteria, that normally mediate social behaviour. Next day one may be embarrassed when reminded of what one said or did. Indeed, there may be little or no recollection of the detailed events that took place when even moderately intoxicated. It is an interesting finding that memory of those events may become available if approximately the same level of blood alcohol or the same degree of intoxication is attained again. It seems that, to some extent, the memories established during an intoxicated state are more readily retrieved, or brought to mind, if that state is re-entered. This type of partial amnesia is not uncommon among 'moderate' or even 'light' drinkers who have consumed enough alcohol to become intoxicated. Loss of memory of this type is different from the 'blackouts' experienced by some 'heavy' drinkers and alcoholics. Blackouts involve a total, or almost total, absence of any memory for events. The drinker may be totally unable to account for his or her movements over a period of hours, or even days. Blackouts are an important warning sign that drinking is excessive. Returning to more moderate drinking, memory for immediate events is also adversely affected. Even in the midst of conventional social drinking, participants are more likely to lose track of what is being said than if they had not been drinking. Attention is more apt to wander, topics of conversation may be changed more frequently and the normal give-and-take of conversation may be replaced by a less well-balanced interaction. The very words and phraseology used in conversation may be altered so that, ultimately, simpler, less complex words and grammatical structures replace more complex ones.

Intellectual performance, as measured by standard psychological tests, is impaired at even low blood alcohol levels, the impairment becoming progressively more severe with increasing alcohol concentration. As indicated, above, the ability to make considered judgements is impaired by alcohol, although small doses may facilitate decision-making. This may be a consequence of reduced anxiety associated with making decisions, or it could be accounted for as an increase in the willingness to take risks. Unfortunately, the impaired judgement and increased willingness to take risks are not noticed by the drinker. The drinker's lack of awareness regarding the presence and extent of these intellectual deficits is typified by the drunken driver's confidence in his or her ability to drive safely. Of course, if that person does drive, there will be impairments in all aspects of driving performance. Thus, alcohol acts in a subtle manner, in that one effect of drinking is an increasingly reduced awareness of the impairments being wrought by that drinking.

Alcohol can increase the drinker's interest in sex and, in modest amounts, may facilitate sexual behaviour. Highly anxious people and, in particular, those who are anxious about sexual activities, are likely to experience deficits in their own sexual performance. Both sexes may suffer a range of such deficits that render sexual intercourse impossible. Although it is not necessary to discuss the mechanisms that bring about this state of affairs, it is enough to know that the physiological processes underlying anxiety can, when anxiety is strong enough, make intercourse physically impossible. Modest alcohol consumption may reduce anxiety, and modify the physiological aspects of anxiety, to such an extent that intercourse does become possible. Unfortunately, if too much alcohol is consumed, the male is likely to experience an 'erectile dysfunction' or 'impotence'. He cannot achieve or maintain an erection, hence, 'intromission' or penetration of his partner, is impossible. Sexual desire is increased while the means of satisfying that desire is reduced in both sexes. Heavy habitual drinking eventually results in a loss of sexual interest, and in males, permanent erectile dysfunction while such drinking continues.

Depressed mood often accompanies continual heavy drinking and is endemic in alcoholics. The drinker is miserable, pessimistic and full of self-doubts. Notice that the 'depressed mood' is not equivalent to clinical 'depression', although the drinker may also be depressed, in the clinical sense. Alcohol-induced depression of mood is frequently intensified by the accumulating personal, social, occupational, health and economic problems that eventually beset habitual excessive drinkers. Given the cognitive impairments, particularly the impaired insight, experienced by such drinkers, they are likely to blame others for the difficulties that they increasingly face. 'Morbid' or abnormal and unreasonable jealousy appears to assail many excessive drinkers, providing yet another source of conflict between partners. This is not to imply that alcohol directly increases some human characteristic called 'jealousy', only that the excessive drinker's total situation makes it more likely that he or she will behave in a jealous manner.

Alcohol is consumed because of the effects it produces in the drinker. More accurately, it is consumed on the basis of its expected positive effects; a matter to be discussed at some length in a later chapter. For the present purposes, let it be agreed that drinkers expect moderate quantities of alcohol to give them a 'lift'. One way in which this might be experienced concerns the drinker's view of him or herself; the self-concept or self-identity. This refers to the total view that the individual has of him or herself. As with most all-encompassing, 'holistic' concepts, the self-concept is multifaceted and complex. In fact, there is no generally accepted way of defining, let alone assessing or measuring, that concept. Leaving aside these conceptual and psychometric difficulties, the concept is useful. If I am asked to describe myself, that description will represent part of my self-concept. The more extensive and encompassing that self-characterization, the closer it will come to being an accurate representation of my self-concept.

There are many ways of assessing the self-concept, each having its strengths and weaknesses, but there is no single widely accepted method. The majority comprise a list of attributes by means of which the individual provides a self-characterization. Most methods also permit the respondent to indicate the extent to which each attribute is present. Self-concept measures typically comprise an extensive list of adjectives, such as: considerate, honest, sympathetic, outspoken and so forth. This type of measure can be used by an individual to depict the self as it is (Actual-self), and as one would ideally like it to be (Ideal-self). Furthermore, the measure can be used to characterize one's perception of another person or people. Thus, it has many uses.

A number of investigations have been carried out into the effects of alcohol on the self-concept of alcoholics and non-alcoholics. The usual procedure is to obtain self-concept characterizations from individuals whose blood alcohol is zero, and to obtain further self-characterizations while those people are drinking and, in some cases, intoxicated. The completed characterizations depict the self-concept changes that occur as a result of drinking and being intoxicated. It has been found that drinking improves the self-concepts of moderate drinkers (Williams 1964), whereas intoxication is associated with a deterioration (Berg 1971; Pollack 1965). In direct contrast, drinking produces a deterioration in alcoholics' self-concept (Vanderpool 1969), while intoxication is associated with an improvement (Berg 1971). On the basis of these findings, one might expect moderate drinkers to avoid, but alcoholics to seek, intoxication.

Technically, 'personality' is a theoretical construct concerning the *relatively* stable behavioural, cognitive, and affective aspects of an individual. The self-concept is, in a sense, the individual's perception of his or her own personality. The description of someone's personality is an attempt to encapsulate the many characteristics within a few words. It is an attempt to understand that person and to make valid predictions about his or her future behaviour. Most important, there is a central assumption that the personality is relatively unaffected by the external environment. According to this assumption, an individual's personality is essentially unchanged, regardless of changes in the person's appearance, circumstances, occupation, status, interests and environment, for example. Most of us will have heard statements of the sort: 'Stan may have gone up in the world but, in spite of that, he's still the same old Stan'. This concept of personality is intuitively appealing since it seems to account for the fact that a person is essentially the 'same' person each time we meet. It would be extremely odd if, each time we met a particular person, he or she had changed to such an extent that we found ourselves wondering whether we were mistaking a succession of strangers for that person. Hence, personality is said to be largely unaffected by the passage of time.

One of the most readily available and socially acceptable ways of producing short-term, or 'acute', changes in personality is by means of psychoactive drugs. These are chemical compounds that affect the psychological processes; prime examples being heroin, LSD and alcohol. There can be no doubt that, in the Western world, the most widely used psychoactive drug is alcohol. The reason that alcohol is so highly valued and has such general social acceptance is that, in modest amounts, it modifies the drinker's personality in ways approved by society. The extent of the modification is dose dependent, and social approval is dependent on the extent and type of modification produced. Long-term heavy and excessive drinking can result in such profound, persistent and adverse personality changes in the drinker that society relegates him or her to the category of 'alcoholic'. The reader will be well aware that this diagnostic label implies many important things. It implies that the alcoholic has habitually and persistently been drinking unusually large quantities of alcohol, that there have been profound personality changes in that person as a consequence of this drinking, and that those changes are socially disapproved.

Drinking and affect

Of all the changes wrought by alcohol, it is probably the drug's ability to modify the emotions that makes it so widely used and valued. A drink can cheer us up, make us feel less anxious, make us more easily amused, more sociable, and so forth. Alcohol makes social events less anxiety-provoking and more enjoyable. Once again, it appears that the anxiety-reducing potential of alcohol is dose dependent. Low blood alcohol concentrations can lead to a reduction in anxiety (Nagarajam *et al.* 1973), whereas higher levels may produce an increase (Mello 1972). On the darker side, impulsiveness, repressed anger, hostility, argumentativeness, feelings of guilt, inferiority, resentment and and so on, may be released by the disinhibiting effects of alcohol. Antisocial behaviour is more likely to erupt when alcohol is being consumed. However, it was pointed out, in the section concerning alcohol and behaviour, that human behaviour is complexly determined. Consequently, well-designed and executed scientific investigations are necessary in order to separate the effects of expectations, social and physical environments, mood and personality; indeed, all the numerous factors that can modify the effects of a drug, from the 'pure', pharmacological effects of the drug. In everyday life, the effects of alcohol on human beings are strongly influenced by the drinker's expectations. If the socially anxious party-goer expects alcohol to make him or her more sociable, outward-going and better able to enjoy and participate in the party, that is likely to be the outcome of drinking. If, however, the same person expects alcohol to make him or her more bluntly outspoken, more easily offended and more aggressive, this is then likely to be the result of drinking. It is the combination of the pharmacological effects of alcohol plus the drinker's expectations, that are the major determinants of the effects of drinking on the individual.

Having emphasized that many factors interact to determine the effects of drinking, it should be recognized that continual, high blood alcohol levels can result in a more-or-less persistent mood change. Mood is progressively and chronically depressed and anxiety may be high. It will be recalled that continued high blood alcohol levels can lead to the phenomenon of tolerance, so that higher doses of the drug are needed in order to produce the effects that, formerly, were achieved at lower doses. At the start of a drinking 'career', alcohol may have been consumed to reduce anxiety and/or depression. Increasing quantities of alcohol are required to achieve the same ends, once tolerance has been established, but anxiety and depression are likely consequences of continual, heavy alcohol intakes. The drinker may well interpret the resurgence of 'bad nerves' as a sign that even higher doses of alcohol are required to produce the desired improvement. Thus, a vicious circle is created. Why does the drinker not recognize what is happening? Many probably do but, by the time things have progressed to this stage, the way back to more moderate drinking may seem too difficult and painful. Social and financial problems may abound at this stage and may appear to be insoluble. The continued use of alcohol is likely to further exacerbate those problems but the drinker's awareness of the latter will be blunted. Under these circumstances, drinking is a means of psychological escape from a wide range of chronic problems.

Chapter 7

Social factors in drinking

In this chapter, the interplay between drinking and inter-personal, familial and social functioning will be briefly reviewed. Brevity is necessary since this is a vast and complex area of inquiry that, given the current context, can only be outlined. One particularly striking feature of this area is that the positive and negative aspects of drinking are probably nowhere more clearly evident. Not the least social consequence of drinking is that it supports a considerable drinks industry. Although this was reviewed in an earlier chapter, it is mentioned here only because the existence of that industry has social consequences for those employed in it.

Non-harmful drinking

The following section concerns drinking that does not give rise to harmful consequences. By now the reader should have a reasonable idea of what is intended by this term.

Social facilitation

Alcohol is widely used to reduce anxiety and tension. Gatherings that would otherwise be anxiety-inducing become less so when alcohol is consumed. For many people, maybe a majority, it would be a daunting prospect to attend a gathering at which they would be expected to socialize with strangers, but at which alcohol was unavailable. A drink can 'break the ice' on such occasions. It has been argued, as will be discussed in the next chapter, that the habitual and heavy use of alcohol for this purpose can lead to problems. Not the least difficulty is that, although alcohol can reduce anxiety and tension, the causes of those unpleasant conditions remain. Alcohol is a palliative, not a cure. Is this really so? The anxious party-goer ceases to feel anxious and tense after a few drinks so, surely, alcohol has provided a cure? The alert reader will already have realized that this question cannot be answered until a definition of the word 'cure' is provided. If, by 'cure' one means that a dose of alcohol, under conditions of social anxiety, results in that anxiety never again being experienced, then alcohol is not a 'cure' but a palliative. Alcohol ameliorates anxiety, at the time, but it does not correct the causes of the anxiety. Thus, on the next similar social occasion, anxiety is no less likely to be experienced. If alcohol is again available, the individual is more likely to use it if it had the desired effects on the previous occasion. Should this pattern of 'chemical coping' be repeated a number of times, it is likely to become a well-established and habitual procedure. For most people this presents no problem, although attending a social gathering at which alcohol is not available may be uncomfortable because the social anxiety is fully felt, rather than 'diluted' with alcohol. The fact remains that the 'tranquillizing' properties of alcohol are highly valued in Western society, although it is not usually thought of in this way. Instead drinkers talk about 'relaxing with a drink' and 'unwinding with a drink'. Finally, although alcohol does probably act as a tension-reducer for most people, there is ample evidence that it can increase tension, anxiety and depression in some alcoholics (see Nathan and O'Brien 1971).

A further feature of drinking in a social context is that,

under some circumstances, and by common consent, social controls are relaxed. In Western society this is most clearly seen during local and national festivals and carnivals. Boisterous, and even aggressive, behaviours are condoned. Sexual mores are relaxed, and social barriers are lowered. It has been reported that some primitive societies hold festivals in which mass drunkenness provides a 'safety valve' for releasing group and individual stresses. Alcohol is used to induce drunkenness that, in such cases, serves a useful social function.

It is worth noting, in passing, that 'drinking' involves much more than swallowing alcohol. The drink has to be obtained, the glass is held and may be manipulated in the hands, the beverage is drunk, the glass held or put down or recharged, and so forth. Each one of these steps can be reduced to a series of events, each of which requires certain intellectual and behavioural skills. Parallel skills are displayed by smokers. One only has to observe the performance of a pipe smoker, to be convinced that this is so. The associated behaviours are an important part of drinking since they may, themselves, serve to reduce tension.

Drinking expectations

The disinhibiting effects of alcohol can, in an appropriate social environment and given appropriate expectations, result in increased conviviality. It is important to appreciate the crucial role played by the social environment and expectations. Alcohol does not, in itself, increase conviviality. If the social environment is convivial, and if the drinker expects alcohol to make him or her more convivial, drinking will probably achieve this end. The social environment indicates what type of behaviour is appropriate or, to express it differently, it sets the scene for particular sorts of behaviour. If, on the other hand, the social environment is convivial but the drinker is having to guard against revealing his or her sadness, drinking may result in the overt expression of that sadness. Some readers will have encountered mildly mannered drinkers who become unaccountably belligerent when they have been drinking. Depending upon the particular individual, one possible explanation relies upon the disinhibiting effects of alcohol. It may be that, under normal circumstances, the mild individual in question is hiding resentful and hostile feelings. These could stem from innumerable sources such as marital conflict, job dissatisfaction, and so forth. When sufficient alcohol has been consumed, the ability to hide these feelings wanes, social inhibitions weaken and, given the appropriate social environment, hostility may be verbally or physically expressed. In this context, the 'appropriate social environment' may be one that is convivial and thus resented, or one that is belligerent and encourages belligerence. The drinker's expectations may be no more than that sufficient alcohol makes people 'run wild', or that drinking frequently leads to fights. The important point is that alcohol can facilitate personally and socially constructive and destructive behaviours. Alcohol does not cause behaviour, in the way that sleeping tablets produce sleep. For example, no jury would be likely to acquit an habitual burglar who claimed, by way of defence, that alcohol 'makes' him commit burglaries. Alcohol might well produce such disinhibition in our burglar that he threw caution to the wind and burgled. It might be that rather than acting 'impulsively' alcohol assuaged his fear of being apprehended. That is to say, drinking alcohol reduced his fears or anxieties about being caught. In fact, the true picture of what caused our burglar to resume his illegal career is likely to be complex, with alcohol playing its part.

Symbolic and ritualistic uses of alcohol

Many people have their first introduction to alcoholic beverages during a family celebration. Christmas, birthdays, weddings, and so forth, provide such opportunities. In many homes, alcohol is rarely available and consumed except at family celebrations. Within the family setting, alcohol serves the same purposes as in other interpersonal and social situations. It may be that the symbolic and ceremonial uses of alcohol are first encountered in the family. Young children see their parents drinking alcoholic beverages and, since the children are likely to be denied access to those beverages, associate drinking with adulthood. Drinking can come to symbolize adulthood and independence. Children may see adults drinking each other's good health, the beverage of choice for this purpose being alcohol. The reason that alcohol is used for this purpose may have something to do with what, to many folk, are its mysterious and almost magical effects on the drinker. To drink to someone's health using alcohol is to use a 'powerful' chemical and, maybe by association and inference, to invoke a powerful 'force' to achieve the desired outcome. Under these circumstances, alcohol has both symbolic and ritual uses. Bargains and 'deals' are sometimes sealed by both parties taking a 'friendly' drink together. An additional function of such drinking could also be to dispel personal and interpersonal tensions that may have arisen in the course of negotiations. Again, it may not have occurred to the reader that alcohol has symbolic and ritual uses in many of the religions of the world.

An important consequence of drinking in the company of others is that group cohesiveness is enhanced. That is to say, one's sense of being part of the group, of 'belonging' in that group, is increased. Of course, this enhanced sense of group cohesiveness can result from a wide range of shared experiences, whether pleasant or unpleasant. Taking meals together tends to enhance closeness and group cohesion, as does supporting the same sports team. On a different level, various 'support' groups have been established by and for the victims of particular types of crime. A large measure of the appeal that such organizations have for the 'new' victim probably stems from the latter's reasonable expectation that fellow victims are likely to be understanding and supportive. Returning to the matter of drinking, it is worth bearing in mind that the sense of cohesiveness that stems from sharing in an activity is enhanced by the pharmacological action of alcohol. We have seen that it can enhance the sense of personal well-being and that it dulls one's critical faculties. The result can be that other people are perceived as being generally more friendly; hence inter-personal attraction and group cohesiveness are enhanced.

Consider, then, the plight of the non-drinker who is in the company of active drinkers. Under such circumstances, the abstainer's behaviour is deviant. Indeed, drinkers may regard the abstainer's refusal to drink as an intentional slight, insult or implied rebuke aimed at them. To decline a drink, without at the same time giving offence, is a social skill that most people are wise enough to acquire in the course of growing up. A major consideration in refusing a drink is to avoid being perceived as 'deviant' and, hence, to remain part of the 'fellowship of drinkers'. One measure of the extent to which drinking is part of everyday life is discernible from the difficulty that abstinent alcoholics have in returning to normal social functioning. They often remark that alcohol is available at a high proportion of social functions. A moment's reflection will confirm the truth of this assertion. The public house is an important traditional social institution in Britain, just as the café is on the Continent. Clubs everywhere derive a significant proportion of their income from the sale of alcohol, many clubs depending on such sales for their continuing existence. Given the widespread availability and use of alcohol, it is clear that not to drink is, indeed, 'deviant'.

Harmful drinking

So far in this chapter the focus has been on 'normal' or socially acceptable drinking. However, excessive drinking provides the very reason for the existence of some groups.

Drinking cliques

It is probably safe to say that most pubs and clubs provide the meeting place of one or more groups of excessive drinkers. This is not to suggest that the casual observer would easily identify such groups. Careful, systematic observations over several weeks would be likely to reveal one or more stable groups of 'heavy', regular drinkers. Of course, not all regular drinkers are also heavy drinkers, just as not all heavy drinkers do so regularly. Heavy, regular drinking cliques are not rarities.

As we have seen in an earlier chapter, young people, as a broad category, tend to be heavier-than-usual drinkers. Experimenting with alcohol, showing one's friends that one can 'hold' drink, and utilizing the disinhibiting effects of alcohol are probably some of the reasons for heavier drinking by this group, leaving aside financial considerations. Is it not curious that the unaided ability to remain vertical, despite having consumed large quantities of alcohol, is seen as confirming the 'tough' status of the drinker?

Occupational drinking

Different motivation for heavy drinking occurs in some occupational groups. Newspaper journalists and photographers, representatives (they used to be referred to as 'travellers'), construction workers and seamen, for example, have amongst their number a higher than usual proportion of heavy drinkers. Each of these occupations involves much travelling or waiting about, hence the public house provides a welcome haven. Recall, too, that alcohol has a high calorific value, so drink may take the place of food. No doubt the reader will be able to complete the rest of the scenario that leads to excessive alcohol intake, dependence and associated disabilities.

Maybe the reader would also care to consider the important question of why only some, rather than all, members of the above occupations succumb to heavy drinking. This question will also be addressed in the next chapter.

The habitual heavy drinker may well exhibit the Alcohol Dependence Syndrome, referred to earlier. Whether or not the 'heavy' drinker suffers from that syndrome, alcohol-related problems are likely to be experienced, some of which will affect the drinker's social functioning.

Drinking and the family

For the current purpose, I shall consider several effects of an individual's excessive drinking on his or her family and friends. These effects start and develop at various points in the development and maintenance phases of excessive drinking. For the sake of simplicity, I shall consider mainly the established alcohol-dependent husband and father, who has a well-developed set of alcohol-related disabilities. This drinker will be referred to as an 'alcoholic'.

The alcoholic, particularly if male, is likely to spend a large part of his leisure time drinking with friends. He may go home after work, but only to leave for the pub at opening time. He may move from one pub to another, or remain in just one until closing time or until he is ejected. Lack of money is overcome be using his skill at getting others to buy him drinks. This probably means that he sees little if anything of his children during the week, and maybe he is drunk when he does. Similarly, at weekends, he is likely to spend much of his time drinking and away from the home. His children have a largely absent father whose mood is unpredictable when he is present. One consequence of this is that the children do not invite their friends home for a meal or to play; they dare not do so lest their father appears in a drunken state. They are ashamed and possibly frightened of him.

His drinking has implications for his children's social functioning. The alcoholic's wife despairs of her husband. He drinks away his income and maybe keeps her short of money. She rarely goes out with her husband because past experience shows that they will come to rest where alcohol is available. She has tried to moderate his drinking by drinking with him, but that never works. The wife may be alienated from her own parental family because, despite their advice, she remains with her husband. She may be alienated from her husband's family if they blame her for his drinking. Friends cannot be invited to the house because the alcoholic may reveal his problem by word or deed so, like her children, the wife of the alcoholic may live a socially deprived existence. Sometimes the wife takes a job to ensure a stable income for bringing up her children. This strategy can easily result in the children being deprived of their mother's company as well as their father's. Sometimes the wife has little alternative but to adopt that course of action, due to the uncertainty of receiving the necessary financial support from her husband.

An understandable but pathetic consequence of the alcoholic's treatment of his family is that the family often conspires to keep their dark secret. They take pains to ensure that the alcoholic's problem remains a family secret, the motivation for this originating in shame, embarrassment, guilt, compassion, denial, and so forth. There is reason to believe that it is unwise to protect the alcoholic from the consequences of his own behaviour. This sort of 'protection' reduces the chances that the alcoholic will seek treatment. In practice, it is often very difficult, and sometimes too difficult, for a wife either to throw her husband out or to take her children and leave him. Threats to do so rarely, if ever, produce a permanent improvement in the alcoholic's behaviour.

It will be clear that the alcoholic and his family are likely to alienate or otherwise lose their non-alcoholic friends. As the drinker's dependence on alcohol increases, he finds that his friends drink 'too slowly', so he becomes intolerant of them. They, for their part, see what is happening and withdraw from what is becoming an aversive relationship. Any attempts by the friends to remain on good terms with the wife are resented by the husband, and she may decide to withdraw from their circle to pacify her husband. Isolation from, or a severe restriction of, normal social relations is the usual lot of the alcoholic and his family. It was pointed out, in an earlier chapter, that much petty crime is committed under the influence of alcohol. It is a grim fact that some families only obtain respite from the consequences of the husband's drinking when he is serving a prison sentence.

'Skid Row'

'Skid Row' alcoholics occupy the far end, the lowest point, of the drinking spectrum. Although they are a small percentage of the total number of alcoholics, they are what most people have in mind when reference is made to 'alcoholics'. The stereotype Skid Row alcoholic is male, middle-aged to elderly, with none of the usual family ties and is socially isolated. He has a long history of alcohol dependence and petty crime, one result of the latter being frequent incarcerations in prison. He is an habitual drunken offender. The Skid Row alcoholic is unlikely ever, either to have had a skilled occupation, or to have been married. He is usually dishevelled, dirty and dressed in a grotesque assortment of old clothes. In winter he wears several top coats, if he can get them, and typically, he stinks. Since most of the money he obtains is spent on alcohol, he eats whatever he can find, and he sleeps rough in derelict houses. As one might expect, these destitute alcoholics sometimes congregate together, particularly in winter, to share a fire and whatever liquor is available. In practice, it is likely to be the cheapest source of alcohol, including methylated spirit, surgical spirit, cider or the cheapest of wines. In British towns and cities the inhabitants of Skid Row are usually distributed widely and thinly throughout. They are not very visible, and do not usually advertise their presence. In contrast, there are usually well-defined, dilapidated and notorious areas in American cities that are the archetypal 'Skid Row'. In general terms, Skid Row represents a degrading way of life from which, once entered, it is extremely difficult to escape. It is the final retreat of those who have themselves rejected, or who have been rejected by society. They are beyond the pale. Maybe it is worth mentioning that not all the inhabitants of Skid Row are alcoholics but a large proportion, at least half, probably are. The routes by which they reach Skid Row will be considered in the next chapter, but such individuals often report a number of social handicaps that reach back into their childhood, and any tenuous commitment they may once have had to society is weakened and destroyed. Excessive drinking ensures that they never establish a place for themselves in normal society. Skid Row is surely the ultimate and most extreme social consequence of drinking. As a general rule, excessive drinking tends to promote downward social mobility. That is to say, the individual's social status tends to deteriorate, as does that of his or her family.

Women and excessive drinking

Before ending this chapter, some reference must be made to the consequences of excessive drinking by women. The alcoholic mother may find her children taken into care or, if divorced, her husband may be granted custody of their children. Again, it is likely that family disintegration is faster and more profound when it is the mother, rather than the father, who is the excessive drinker. Overall, there can be no reasonable doubt that female alcoholics are regarded in an even worse light than are their male counterparts. Society's response to the female alcoholic is the more severe as a consequence. Interestingly, the systematic study of excessive drinking by females is a relatively recent phenomenon. One reason is probably that the full extent of such drinking is only now becoming · evident. The social climate is such that women are now more ready to divulge their drinking practices and problems. Could another reason for this dearth of information about female drinking and drinking problems arise from a reluctance, in the past, on the part of male research workers to broach such an 'indelicate' subject?

Chapter 8

Explanations of drinking and alcoholism

By this point, the reader will be well aware of the problems associated with definitions. Thus, the title of this chapter refers to 'drinking' and 'alcoholism', despite both terms being ambiguous. It is worth reiterating that by 'drinking' I am referring to so called 'social' or 'non-problem' drinking that rarely, if ever, leads to even transient difficulties. This is the type of drinking enjoyed by the vast majority of people. Conversely, by 'alcoholism' I mean the 'alcohol-dependence syndrome', with or without 'alcohol-related disabilities'. Between these two types of alcohol usage there is a grey area into and out of which some people move. This is the area of greater or lesser overlap. In what follows there is no suggestion that aspects of the explanations included under the heading of 'drinking' cannot be applied to 'alcoholism', or the other way round. One should always remember that the alcoholic had to become a 'drinker' before becoming an 'alcoholic'. Current opinion is that 'drinking' and 'alcoholism' are not utterly different, but are different points on a single continuum.

Before turning to the main subject matter of this chapter it is as well to consider what a 'good' explanation should provide. Unfortunately, philosophers of science are not in full agreement over this question, so we shall have to be content with only a rough outline. I would suggest that, in general terms, a good explanation of drinking, and alcoholism would account for the onset (or aetiology) for maintenance, and for change. In the case of drinking, a good explanation would indicate why people begin to drink in the first instance, why they continue to do so, why they vary their drinking behaviour, and why they cease to drink. In the case of alcoholism, a good explanation would account for the transition from 'drinking' to 'alcoholism', it would explain the maintenance and course of alcoholism, and it would elucidate the processes by which change occurs. This latter would include both the exacerbation and amelioration of the condition. A moment's reflection will suggest that this is asking a great deal of a single theory, given the complexity of the behaviours under consideration. In fact, there is general agreement that unidimensional, simple explanations are unlikely to prove useful. The current position is that complex human behaviours require complex, multidimensional explanations. Drinking and alcoholism are likely to be understood best in terms of complex interactions between organic, psychological and sociological variables. I am not suggesting that unidimensional explanations are 'useless', only that they can, at best, provide part of the 'complete' explanation. It is important to keep these caveats in mind whilst reading the remainder of this chapter.

Drinking

The most general statement that can be made about how people begin their drinking 'careers' is that society encourages and teaches them to do so. The process will be familiar to most readers, and forms part of the process known as 'socialization', or learning to be an acceptable member of one's society. The family is the most influential force in the individual's early years, and it is usually in the family that the child first encounters the use of alcohol. The parents, siblings, relatives and visitors provide examples, or 'models', for the child. If the child is exposed to moderate drinking models, he or she is likely to accept that as the normal and desirable pattern for adults. In most families, the child learns that only adults are legally allowed to buy and drink alcohol. Drinking thereby becomes a symbol of adult status, alongside other symbols such as smoking, driving vehicles on the public highway, working for a living, and so on. A study carried out in Glasgow by Jahoda and Cramond (1972) found that about 40 per cent of six-year-old children could identify alcoholic drinks by their smell alone, whilst some 60 per cent had acquired this ability by the age of 10 years. It was further shown that, by the age of six years, 40 per cent had tasted alcohol and had encountered drunken adults. By eight years of age, most children had mastered the concept of 'alcohol'. They recognized the special status of alcohol as a drink, and had formed the association between alcohol and certain maladaptive or socially unacceptable adult behaviours. One particularly interesting finding of this study was although most young children have a neutral or moderately favourable attitude towards alcohol, this tends to become more negative between the ages of six and ten years. The authors suggested that this negative attitude probably results from the child learning that school teachers and the church do not approve of alcohol. The early influence of the family declines as the child encounters authority figures at school and elsewhere.

The important influence of peer pressure was indicated by a further study in Glasgow by Davies and Stacey (1972). Their investigation of alcohol use amongst 14 to 17-year-olds showed that peer pressure becomes the dominant influence during those years. By the age of 14 years, 92 per cent of boys and 85 per cent of girls had tasted alcohol. Their former, pre-adolescent rather negative attitudes towards alcohol had reversed, the abstainer being construed as unsociable and weak, while the drinker was regarded as sociable and tough. It was between the ages of 14 and 17 years that regular drinking became established in response to the drinking model provided by their friends. In addition to being seen as socially desirable, drinking bestowed prestige on the drinker. Importantly, heavy drinking was regarded as being socially undesirable. Most males claimed to be drinking in public houses by the age of 17 years, whilst most females drank either in public houses or in dance halls. Both sexes were drinking below the age at which they could legally do so in public bars. A more recent study of 13 to 18-year-olds conducted in England by Hawker (1978) confirmed the early teenage drinking habits reported in the Glaswegian studies.

It was pointed out in an earlier chapter that the heaviest drinkers are unmarried males in their late teens and early twenties. On the whole, this group has a higher than average spending power, has no family commitments and engages in activities that are associated with drinking. Thus, drinking is an important feature of their socializing, and a way of bolstering self-confidence at an age when, for many, it is being put under severe strain. Official statistics show that young males are more likely than anyone else to be arrested by the police for drink-associated offences. High alcohol intakes are associated with increased drink-related problems. Fortunately, moderate drinking is the norm amongst young people and, usually, even those who do drink excessively markedly reduce their intake when they marry and set up home. Serious, long-term problems occur when young people fail to develop interests and activities that preclude excessive drinking. Under those circumstances drinking may remain the paramount focus of their social activities. As their peers take up other commitments and withdraw from the heavy-drinking group, there remains a hard core of heavy drinkers. The latter tends to draw closer together, and become confirmed in that drinking style, with the attendant risk to each participant that he may eventually exhibit the alcohol-dependence syndrome and develop further alcohol-related problems. Drinking is a central factor in the heavy drinker's lifestyle. With the exception of lone drinkers, that lifestyle involves spending a large proportion of their spare time with other heavy drinkers. One can appreciate that a group of this sort provides social support and a role or identity. The group serves an important function for its members.

Returning to the question of age-related drinking patterns, there is a general expectation that they will be more moderate in middle age than in youth, and that they will be yet more restrained in the elderly. The middle-aged are expected to drink in moderation, to stay out of drink-related trouble, and to use alcohol for pleasant social facilitation. That these expectations are fulfilled by the majority of middle-aged people is common knowledge. Likewise, the elderly are expected to drink moderately, making their drinks last. Hence, they are unlikely to use a public house or club that attracts a lot of potentially noisy young people. The typical elderly person is thought of as enjoying a 'quiet drink'. It hardly needs to be pointed out that we all, in part, derive these several expectations from observing the behaviour of different age groups. Their behaviours will be influenced by a variety of factors, as indicated above, many, if not all of which, change with the age of the drinker. One comes full circle with the realization that although our expectations arise in part from observing drinkers' behaviours, those very behaviours are influenced by society's expectations, of which for the most part, our expectations are a part.

Drinking behaviour is not static but usually changes throughout the individual's life. Most youthful heavy drinkers eventually become elderly 'quiet' drinkers. Some do not, and some drinkers from all age groups develop excessive drinking habits. It is to these that we now turn.

Alcoholism

It is almost certainly true to say that the majority of

research carried out on the consumption of alcohol by human beings has been concerned with damaging drinking, or what I shall refer to as 'alcoholism'. The reasons for this preoccupation with alcoholism will probably be self-evident, so they will not be reviewed in detail; however, some mention of them must be made for the sake of completeness. The harmful personal, interpersonal and social consequences of excessive drinking have been recognized for centuries, so alcoholism has long been a matter of public concern. Law enforcement and custodial agencies have been interested to the extent that alcoholics have traditionally been committed to prison when they offended. Inevitably, prison has not deterred alcoholics from drinking, so in recent years law enforcement and more particularly custodial agencies have become more concerned with cure than mere custody. Therapists have been interested in alcoholism, since it is they who have been called upon to treat the condition. Theoreticians in the medical, physiological, psychological and social sciences have been interested in alcoholism, not least because it presents fascinating and complex problems for these disciplines. As one might expect, the different general orientations of these disciplines have given rise to theories that are appropriate to those orientations. Sociologists produce sociological theories, biochemists produce biochemical explanations of alcoholism. Beyond even this level of complexity, each discipline has engendered a clutch of theories, depending upon the particular theoretical orientations of their originators. Under these circumstances it is important to keep in mind the caution mentioned at the beginning of this chapter. Complex human behaviours require complex multidimensional (or multidisciplinary) explanations. Each discipline has its own perspective on alcoholism. In general, the better a theory is, the more of the observed facts it is able to account for. It is not appropriate to criticize a sociological theory of alcoholism for failing to explain biochemical data, for example. It is appropriate to question the 'completeness' or 'explanatory power' of such a theory for being unable to explain a social aspect of alcoholism. The point being emphasized is that each discipline has its part to play in understanding alcoholism, but such understanding is not the sole prerogative of any one discipline.

In the remainder of this chapter I shall review theories that reflect organic, psychological and sociological perspectives.

Organic theories

Genetic

There is an age-old observation that when one member of a family is an excessive drinker, one or more relatives are also likely to have a drinking problem. Excessive drinking seems to run in families, and may not be confined to one generation. This has given rise to the view that alcoholism may be inherited. A different but equally likely explanation would be that the child learns to drink excessively by following the example of the alcoholic relatives. This child learns to be an alcoholic. Testing these alternative hypotheses is more difficult than one might anticipate. Leaving aside these difficulties, Goodwin and his colleagues (1973, 1974, 1977) have provided some important findings concerning alcoholism and heredity. They conducted a series of studies in Denmark, making use of the excellent public health records maintained in that country.

Adults who had had at least one alcoholic parent were carefully selected and interview. Some of the subjects had been raised by their biological parents, others had been adopted soon after birth, by non-related non-alcoholic parents. It was found that, whether or not they were raised by their alcoholic parents or by non-alcoholic foster parents, the sons of alcoholics were about four times more likely to develop alcoholism than were the sons of non-alcoholic parents. The number of sons involved was substantial, so these findings strongly suggest an inherited predisposition towards alcoholism. A later (1977) but similar study on adult daughters produced similar results, also indicating a fourfold increase in the expected alcoholism rate, when compared to women whose parents were not alcoholic. The main problem with this study was the small number of inter-viewed daughters who were diagnosed alcoholic. Even so, like the earlier studies, the results suggest that a genetic susceptibility to develop alcoholism was present in the daughters of alcoholics. Furthermore, it appears that daughters may be as genetically susceptible to alcoholism as are sons. Goodwin and his colleagues speculated that the lower female alcoholism rates may be a consequence of society, or their own biological make-up, providing extra protection for them.

It is important that the results of these and other genetic findings are properly understood. All the studies that have investigated the heritability of alcoholism have shown that only a minority of the sons and daugh-ters of alcoholic parents themselves become alcoholic. An inherited susceptibility is a susceptibility, but no more than that. The point was made earlier, and will be made again, that alcoholism has many causes that come together in complex ways to impinge upon the individual. Assuming, as now appears to be the case, that heredity sometimes plays a role in the development of alcoholism, it cannot 'force' a drinker to become an alcoholic. The sons and daughters of alcoholics need not fear that they are 'doomed' to become alcoholics themselves. As a group, they seem to be susceptible, but that statement implies nothing about the individual.

Biochemical

Silkworth, a physician and staunch supporter of Alcoholics Anonymous in its early days, proposed that alcoholism results from an allergy. This theory suggests that, as a result of their physical constitution, some people are 'allergic' to alcohol. This allergy is said to exist prior to the individual ever drinking alcohol. Unfortunately, once the person has consumed alcohol the allergic reaction results in a craving for more alcohol and the development of dependence on alcohol. Alcoholics may be attracted to this theory for many reasons, but two could be salient. First, it declares that alcoholism is a disease like other diseases; thus, the individual's feelings of guilt may be assuaged. Second, it appears to fit the experience of those many members of Alcoholics Anonymous who recall that their drinking was never 'normal': it was always 'alcoholic' from the first sip, in the same way that alcohol and drinking had always had a special significance for the individual.

Several theories have been advanced in which metabolic deficiencies are said to be the cause of alcoholism. For example, one postulates that alcoholics are individuals who have been born with an enzyme deficiency. This results in a reduced ability to metabolize certain nutrients. According to this theory, alcohol alleviates or satisfies the need for those substances, hence a need for alcohol is established. The alcoholic is someone who must drink to excess in order to counteract an inherited enzyme disorder. Research has failed to detect any inherited enzyme deficiency in alcoholics, and there is no evidence that alcohol was craved before the onset of the alcohol-dependence syndrome.

Rather than continuing to list defunct biochemical theories of alcoholism, it is enough to say that none has so far received the empirical support necessary for it to be considered as a serious contender. Typically, alcoholics have been examined, with the result that various biochemical or metabolic disturbances have been observed in some of the sample. Attempts have been made to explain these findings, sometimes by noting similarities between the symptoms of alcoholism and those of conditions in which similar biochemical or

metabolic abnormalities are known to exist. The limitations of the original observations are easily overlooked,
albeit inadvertently, and a new theory is launched.

Before proceeding further, a simple yet crucial point
must be made about all attempts to explain alcoholism,
and any other human or animal disorder. Whenever a
group with a designated disorder is investigated and
found to be significantly different, in some respect, from
most non-disordered members of the same species, the
first question to be answered must be whether that
detected difference is a cause or a consequence of the
disorder. To take a foolish example, many alcoholics
have poor nutritional habits. It is known that this results
from dietary neglect by the individual, partly because
alcohol may be supplying the major proportion of the
alcoholic's calorie intake. If this was not known to be the
case, someone might well have argued that alcoholics
drink excessively to forget their antipathy for food. An
alternative might be that the unhappiness reported by
many alcoholics is a consequence of their subconscious
antipathy for food and resulting self-destructive drinking.
The simple point is that cause and effect must be distinguished although, under some circumstances, cause and
effect can enter into a circular relationship.

Brain damage

It has long been known that, following brain damage,
some individuals drink excessively. This has given rise to
the speculation that alcoholism may be a consequence of
undetected brain damage in those who subsequently
become alcoholics. Evidence of brain damage has been
discovered, *post mortem*, in many alcoholics and, in the
midst of life, some alcoholics display symptoms that are
associated with brain damage. There are several problems
with this appealing theory. The concept of 'brain damage'
is too vague to be very useful. Damage of different parts
or areas of the brain is associated with different or sometimes overlapping sets of symptoms. 'Damage to the

brain' can have very diverse consequences. A theory that suggests 'brain damage' as the cause of alcoholism must also specify the location and nature of the damage. Most importantly, it must identify the resulting disruptions of brain functions, in addition to explaining how these disrupted functions gave rise to excessive drinking in the first instance. No 'brain damage theory to alcoholism' begins to satisfy these requirements.

Psychological theories

Psychoanalytic

According to psychoanalytic theorists, alcoholism results from fixation at the oral stage to psychosexual development. This basic general position has given rise to a variety of specific viewpoints, two only of which will be outlined here. According to Knight (1937), many male alcoholics report that, when they were young, their mothers were excessively protective towards them. Knight hypothesized that the alcoholic developed an enduring psychological need to remain dependent as a result of this early experience. As the child grew, however, he was encouraged to become independent. This frustration produced anger, hostility and guilt over these negative feelings, and over his desire to remain dependent. Excessive drinking enables the alcoholic to control the dependency needs and to retaliate against those who deny him affection. A contrary view was provided by Fenichel (1945). According to this theorist, alcoholics were not overprotected by their mothers. They were rejected or neglected to such an extent that they looked to their fathers, instead. Unconscious homosexual impulses resulted from this orientation of the child towards his father, but these impulses were repressed before they could gain overt expression. Not to be fully denied, these powerful but repressed impulses led the alcoholic to seek male company in bars, in an effort to gain emotional solace that is denied to him by women.

Although the psychoanalytic explanation of alcoholism is intellectually appealing, it is overinclusive. It is a very general explanation, but not one that is able to explain why some people develop alcoholism whilst others do not. The early childhood experiences reported by alcoholics and their apparent 'immaturity' are not specific to alcoholism: they are found across a wide range of psychopathological states. A further particularly damaging objection is that the theory is untestable. In science, it is a widely accepted principle that theories must be testable and open to disproof. If the explanatory power of a theory cannot be tested, that theory is of minimal use to science. The psychoanalytic explanation of alcoholism is not testable in any way that would satisfy the scientific community at large.

Power need

McClelland *et al.* (1972) denied the classic psychoanalytic view that alcoholism results from dependency needs, proposing instead that all drinking stems from a need for power. Alcoholics are said to be individuals who have a particularly strong need for personal power; thus they drink excessively to achieve that sense of power. McClelland and his colleagues have carried out experimental studies, the results of which they believe to support the theory. At least four questions still remain to be answered. Is the excessive power need characteristic of all male alcoholics? Is the excessive power need characteristic of female alcoholics and, indeed, all female alcoholics? What causes this excessive need for power in the first instance? Finally, why do alcoholics turn to alcohol, rather than goal-directed striving, to satisfy their power need?

Transactional analysis

Transactional analysis (Berne 1964) is an approach that seeks to understand human behaviour in terms of interpersonal interactions. A fundamental contention of this model is that, under some circumstances, people engage in complex interpersonal interactions whose ulterior motive is to obtain interpersonal advantage. The convert motive for participating in these manoeuvres is to receive some valued 'pay-off'. According to this viewpoint, alcoholism is best understood, not in terms of organic, psychological or social pathologies, but as a 'game', in the above sense. I shall outline one 'game' that alcoholics are alleged to 'play', so that the reader gains insight into this approach. One of the simplest games involves self-destruction of the body. The alcoholic drinks excessively, eats an inadequate diet, sustains internal organ damage, suffers physical damage, and so on. Clearly, this individual is incapable of looking after him or herself, so others come forward to assume that responsibility. Typically, this alcoholic is taken into medical care, is hospitalized, nurtured and provided with accommodation. The 'game' is one of making other people assume responsibility for the alcoholics's welfare. Other, much more complex 'games' have also been identified by transactional analysts.

Those who work in the area of alcoholism recognize that the transactional approach does provide a way of understanding the condition. One can interpret much of the alcoholic's behaviour in terms of 'games' and 'pay-offs', and so forth. The difficulty is that the transactional model is based upon the established alcoholic's current behaviour. It is a useful framework with which to understand current interactions but it does not explain the genesis of alcoholism. The same criticism also applies to the transactional explanations of the psychopathologies, in general.

Behavioural

In its simplest form, the behavioural explanation construes alcoholism as a set of behaviours that are maintained by their consequences. The consequences 'reinforce' the drinking behaviour; that is to say, they strengthen and maintain drinking. If, for instance, the individual enjoys the taste of the drink and/or the effects of drinking, then he or she is likely to drink again at some time. Drinking is reinforced by its consequences. If the taste was unpleasant and the effects disliked, drinking is not reinforced and, therefore, is less likely to occur again. Again, if the anxious person discovers that alcohol reduces that anxiety, he or she is likely to drink when next assailed by anxiety. According to this conceptualization, drinking at a social gathering is reinforcing; it is advantageous to the drinker. It may reduce social anxiety, allow the individual to feel more physically relaxed, take the 'edge' off his or her shyness, make others seem more amusing, friendly and less threatening, and so on. Whilst the reader may be willing to accept the behavioural model at this level, some may object that the disastrous consequences of drinking severely argue against its applicability to most alcoholics. When excessive drinking is manifestly so damaging, how can the behavioural model then be valid? One advantage with the behavioural model is that it is easily able to cope with this objection, because it can accommodate changing circumstances. A hypothetical case should serve to make this clear.

Suppose that Mr X becomes a drinker in the way most people do, during his teenage years. During this period, the valued consequences of drinking may include gaining approval from his peers for being a drinker among drinkers, feeling more relaxed and self-confident in social situations that would otherwise provoke anxiety, and self-approval for being a 'drinking man'. These are but a few of the many possible reinforcing consequences of drinking. Suppose that Mr X is painfully shy in the company of girls. He may begin to drink more heavily to assuage his shyness and to feel more self-confident. If this method of coping with interpersonal anxiety becomes well established, it is likely to be used for an ever-widening range of stressful interpersonal situations.

Maybe Mr X. starts his own small business, working long hours and using alcohol to relax and, sometimes having missed a meal, as a food substitute. He may have to meet clients to negotiate business deals, fortifying himself before the meeting with a drink, and drinking to close the deal afterwards. If married, he may incur the resentment of his wife for always working and for being away from home for so much of the time. One way in which Mr X may cope with marital tensions is by drinking. Over an extended period, and in response to many different circumstances and pressures, drinking may become his preferred coping strategy, and this is likely to be associated with an increasing habitual intake.

Eventually, Mr X may become physiologically addicted to alcohol, so that unless he keeps 'topped up', he experiences withdrawal symptoms and ceases to function satisfactorily. Drinking is necessary to get through the day and to avoid withdrawal symptoms. Others may realize that he is drinking too much and deteriorating in a variety of personal, interpersonal, social and economic ways, but this may not be at all clear to Mr X. Recall that his judgment will be impaired by alcohol. On the other hand, he may recognize his dependence on alcohol, believing that alcohol itself is the one thing that keeps him functioning despite his 'bad nerves', his lack of appetite for food, his disturbed sleep, and his nagging wife. By now his wife is likely to be at loggerheads with her husband over his drinking. She may be kept short of money and their children may therefore be inadequately fed and clothed. She may have an affectionate husband and father increasingly neglecting his family and business to drink, despite promises from him that he will moderate his alcohol intake. From an objective point of view, Mr X's drinking is destroying him, his family and his business. If the behavioural model is to stand, it must be able to accommodate these facts by suggesting how the costs to Mr X are outweighed by the benefits of excessive drinking.

Although Mr X might never try to formulate the equation, if he did so it might run as follows. On the 'debit' side he is physiologically and psychologically addicted to alcohol, he may have sustained organic damage as a result of drinking, his intellectual ability is impaired, he no longer functions as a normal member of society, he is alienated from his family and non-alcoholic friends, his business is foundering, he is in financial straits, and he can see no solution to his problems. On the 'credit' side, Mr X probably believes that only alcohol keeps him functioning. It enables him to avoid withdrawal symptoms, it enables him to endure his nagging wife and demanding family, and it allows him to blame his competitors and customers for the demise of his business. If, from time to time, Mr X does reduce his drinking, he may be so overwhelmed when he recognizes the parlous state he has reached that he rapidly returns to excessive drinking to ease his conscience, ameliorate his anxiety, and generally 'enable him to live with himself'.

This hypothetical example is by no means an exaggeration, but is an attempt to provide a *simplified* sketch of how the alcohol-dependence syndrome and alcohol-related problems can gradually develop. It is said that there are as many routes to alcoholism as there are alcoholics. The behavioural model is able to accommodate the initiation, development, maintenance and recovery from alcoholism. The basic model is very simple but can accommodate the complexities that are found in the real world of alcoholism. Unfortunately, it is not predictive, except at the most general level. It cannot be used to predict whether or not an individual will become an alcoholic. It does recognize the uniqueness of the individual, and provides a conceptual framework for understanding what is, to many people, the inexplicable behaviour of the alcoholic. More important, the behavioural model provides a framework for therapy. Excessive drinking is said to be maintained by its consequences for the alcoholic. Once the therapist understands the events that precipitate and the consequences that maintain excessive drinking, a remedial programme can be developed to suit the particular alcoholic in question.

Tension reduction

The complexity and multidimensional causation of alcoholism was emphasized in discussing the most recent behavioural model of alcoholism. The precise function served by excessive drinking varies from one alcoholic to another, and it may serve many functions for a particular individual. Thus, there is unlikely to be a single reason for an alcoholic's drinking. Attempts have been made to identify single, universal causes, a much researched one being tension reduction. It was suggested that alcoholics use alcohol as a means of coping with unpleasantly high levels of tension. This makes good sense from a moderate drinker's standpoint, because it is one socially accepted function of drinking. Many alcoholics report experiencing high levels of tension and anxiety, and typi___ alcohol helps them ___

On the face ___ appealing ___ hy___

rienced negative mood changes. The behavioural model provides a framework through which to discover the answer. They continued to drink because, despite the negative mood changes, drinking continued to be reinforcing. Expressed in different terms, it was in their interests to continue drinking. The precise function of the drinking, the purpose it served, could only have been determined by a careful functional analysis. At this distance in time from the experiment, one can do no more than speculate about the functional significance of their drinking, but even that may be instructive. The 10 alcoholic subjects were in hospital throughout the study. Thus, they were accommodated, fed, allowed access to alcohol, were given a great deal of attention by the staff, and were notorious 'celebrities' from the point of view of the other patients. Attention and status may have been the reinforcers that maintained their drinking. Group reinforcement) among the alcoholics may hile it may also have 'machismo' or of these

...y claim that ...ope with these unpleasant feelings. ...of it, the 'tension-reduction hypothesis' is ...g, and animal studies have usually supported the ...pothesis (Hodgson *et al*. 1979). This promising picture is upset by the fact that some alcoholics experience an increase in tension and anxiety as a consequence of drinking.

Mendelson *et al*. (1964) selected 10 alcoholics who claimed that drinking reduced their tensions. The effects of drinking on their self-reported mood states were studied during a 24-day experimental period. Despite the claims they made before the start of the study, at no point during the study did their mood improve. Most damagingly for the tension-reduction hypothesis, anxiety, depression and aggressiveness increased during the last 19 days of the study. Hence, the tension-reduction hypothesis was not supported by the results of this experiment.

It is instructive to consider the question why those 10 alcoholics continued to drink even though they expe-

pressure (socia̶l̶.̶.̶.̶.̶.̶.̶
have maintained their drinking, wh̶i̶.̶.̶.̶
served to strengthen their self-perceived i̶.̶.̶.̶
their public image as 'hard men'. If even one o̶.̶.̶.̶
hypothesized 'pay-offs' outweighed the negative con̶.̶.̶.̶
quences of continuing to drink, one can see that drinking
would be likely to continue. A particular strength of the
behavioural model is that it can be tested. Hence the
above hypotheses could have been tested at the time of
the study, although unfortunately, they were not.

Loss of control and craving

As a result of the findings from a survey which he
conducted on members of Alcoholics Anonymous,
Jellinek (1952) concluded that whenever an alcoholic
consumes alcohol, however little, the ability to choose
when to stop drinking is lost. There is a loss of control
over drinking, and cessation occurs only when the individual is too drunk or sick to drink any more. Experimental evidence does not support this view. Marlatt *et
al.* (1973) tested the 'priming' effects of alcohol on

alcoholics. Two groups of alcoholics were given an initial drink, that of the first group containing alcohol, that of the second containing none. The same masking flavour was included in all the drinks to prevent their true nature being detected. Half of each group was told that their drink did contain alcohol, half were told that it did not. Thus, half who actually drank alcohol believed their drink to be alcohol free, whereas half who did not drink alcohol believed their drink did contain alcohol. According to the loss of control hpothesis, those subjects who had consumed alcohol should then have gone on to drink heavily. In the event, when given access to alcohol, no priming effect was observed, regardless of the content of the initial drink. However, the alcoholics who *believed* they had been given alcohol did drink more than those who had the opposite belief. No loss of control was observed. Hodgson *et al.* (1979) used a more sensitive measure of drinking and did find a priming effect in severely alcohol-dependent subjects. Again, no loss of control was observed. The available evidence from well-conducted research studies indicates that the loss of control phenomenon is a myth.

The same team of researchers manipulated 'craving' for alcohol in alcoholics. A 'low craving' group was denied alcohol for half-an-hour and a 'high craving' group was kept without alcohol for three hours. Data were collected from both groups at the start of the experiment, and after one, two and three hours. After three hours, there was a greater wish to drink, a greater difficulty in resisting alcohol, and greater anxiety in the 'high craving' group. It was also shown that this group drank more quickly immediately after the experimental period than they did before it. The concept of craving was supported by these findings. Despite the clarity of these findings, it must be borne in mind that the alcoholic subjects were being observed and knew they were being observed. The drinking situation was 'artificial' in that sense. The fact remains that there is overwhelming evidence from laboratory and ecological studies (observing alcoholics in the 'real' world) that alcoholics can and do control their drinking under some circumstances. They do sometimes slow down, stop, or speed up their drinking, for longer or shorter periods, depending upon a wide variety of circumstances. Recall the overriding importance of the alcoholic's beliefs about the composition of his drink, in the study by Marlatt *et al.* (1973). It is possible that alcoholics who believe the loss of control hypothesis may, indeed, 'lose control'. If so, they would appear to be acting out a pernicious myth.

Personality

The extensive search for the 'alcoholic personality' has been fruitless. It can be stated with confidence that there is no special set of personality characteristics that is to be found in all alcoholics. This much is certain. This is not to deny that some alcoholics display abnormal personality characteristics, but this may well be a consequence of alcohol abuse. Given that no single 'core' alcoholic personality exists, the question becomes one of whether certain characteristics of personality predispose individuals to become alcoholics. The type of research needed to answer that question is long-term, prospective and expensive. Fortunately, studies of this sort have been carried out in North America. The Oakland Growth Study was initiated in the 1930s in California. A large, randomly selected sample of children was subjected to detailed study, and was followed up at intervals over the next 30 years or so. At the onset, and throughout the study, information about the individual subjects was obtained from a variety of sources, including parents, teachers, peers and self-report. Jones (1968, 1971), reported the mid-1960s findings. Adult male problem drinkers showed some of their characteristic traits that had been present in adolescence. They were extrovert, impulsive, and had a 'tough' or 'machismo' style of self-presentation. In high school they had been more sensitive to criticism, less calm, less academically productive, and less socially aware than was the norm for their group. The results for women were less clear-cut but certain high-school traits persisted into adulthood, including social withdrawal, dependence, irritability, and sensitivity to criticism. In broad terms, these male and female personality characteristics could be seen as indicative of relatively poor social adjustment. In males, they were associated with heavy drinking, in females with *either* heavy drinking *or* abstinence. Returning to the theme of multi-dimensional causation that has been propounded throughout this chapter, it is reasonable to expect personality to play some part in the making of an alcoholic, but personality is one factor amongst many.

Socio-cultural theories

In this last part of the chapter I shall consider some social, cultural, religious, ethnic and family factors that have been identified as possible contributory causes of alcoholism.

McCord *et al.* (1960) followed up a sample of young American males who had been subjected to close scrutiny as adolescents. Two factors, ethnicity and social class, differentiated those who developed alcoholism from those who did not. Those from American Indian, Irish and Western or Eastern European backgrounds were more likely to become alcoholics than those of Latin extraction. Likewise, middle-class adolescents were more likely to become alcoholics than their lower-class peers. There are some difficulties over this study.

Ireland has one of the lowest alcoholism rates in the EEC, and Italy has the second highest. Notice that the majority of subjects in McCord *et al*'s study were not living in their country of ethnic origin. There is increasing reason to believe that such groups are subject to higher rates of social and psychological problems than is the indigenous population.

Whilst it is well established that the per capita alcohol consumption and rates of alcohol-related problems vary from one country to another, there is ample evidence of parallel variations at the regional level. Kilich and Plant (1981) reviewed official figures from a wide variety of sources, and found considerable regional variations in the levels of alcohol-related problems. For example, the overall rates of alcohol-related problems were higher in Scotland and Northern Ireland, than in Wales and Southern England. Interestingly, unemployment rates and alcoholism hospital admission rates showed strong positive associations in Scotland, England and Wales. Even at sub-regional level, relations between residential location and drinking have been found. Urban dwellers are more likely to drink, and to drink more heavily than their small-town and rural counterparts.

Religious affiliation appears to be associated with drinking and drinking problems. Moslems and Mormons, who are forbidden alcohol, have low alcoholism rates, although not zero rates. Orthodox Jews have similarly low rates, partly it is claimed because heavy drinking and drunkenness are frowned upon. Also, children are introduced to the use of alcohol in the family setting at mealtimes and as part of the family's religious observations. It appears that there is a relatively higher proportion of heavy drinkers among Roman Catholics than amongst Protestants. Why this is so is not clear, although many Catholic countries are also wine producers and, on the whole, alcohol consumption is relatively higher amongst producing countries.

It will be recalled that Chapter 4 of this book contains some results from the recent survey into drinking in England and Wales (Wilson 1980a). The original report contains many findings concerning drinking patterns and associated sociocultural factors. Interested readers are referred to Chapter 4, and, for those who thirst after the full story, to the original report. Likewise, Chapter 4 also contains a discussion of the relations between certain occupations and the drinking practices of those engaged in those occupations.

Conclusions

The important point to emerge from this chapter is that many perspectives can be brought to bear on drinking and alcoholism. It is unrealistic to imagine that any one can provide a 'complete' understanding of these complex phenomena. Multidimensional explanations are necessary. The determinants of an individual's drinking behaviour, whether the latter is benign or 'pathological', are many in number and will vary between individuals. It is for this reason, among others, that treating alcoholics and preventing relapses is no easy task.

Chapter 9

Treatment by whom, where and towards what goals?

A wide variety of professionals and non-professionals have an interest in the field of alcoholism. Alcohol abolitionists, members of Alcoholics Anonymous, the drinks industry, employers, educators, legislators, the police, therapists, and so on, all have varying degrees of interest and, it can be anticipated, differing perspectives on the subject. Ask members of these groups about practical solutions to drinking problems and, obviously, the answer provided would depend on the respondent's orientation. The abolitionist would point out that alcoholism cannot exist in the absence of alcohol; so abolish the sale of alcohol and make it a punishable offence to consume the stuff. The health educator might suggest continual nationwide programmes aimed at preventing alcoholism in the first instance, together with parallel programmes encouraging alcoholics to confront their problem and to seek help in overcoming it. Yet again, the police might emphasize the futility of jailing 'habitual drunkenness offenders', whilst therapists might focus on treatment. The object of this chapter will be to examine a range of issues related to treatment.

Spontaneous remission versus treatment

Spontaneous remission refers to the phenomena of

recovery without benefit of treatment. Most readers will have experienced aches and pains that 'just went'. Many conditions, organic, psychological, interpersonal and social, do remit spontaneously, a fact that must be taken into consideration when evaluating any therapeutic endeavour. The question is not so much whether a treatment is effective, but whether it is more effective than no treatment at all. If a treatment is less effective than no treatment at all, then it is harmful, and there would be grounds for not employing that 'treatment'.

There is a problem with the term 'spontaneous'. 'Spontaneous' implies that remission is automatic, or takes place without the intervention of an external agency. Hence, to claim that drinking problems can sometimes remit spontaneously suggests that those problems somehow disappear of their own accord. This proves not to be so. Tuchfeld (1981) intensively interviewed 51 people, some of whom were alcoholics, whose problem drinking had remitted spontaneously an average of about six and a half years before the start of the study. A wide variety of circumstances initiated the individual's commitment to resolve his or her drinking problems. These included a rejection of the label 'alcoholic' and a distaste for formal, institutionalized treatment, the occurrence of a personally humiliating event, the onset of a serious health problem, extensive exposure to information regarding the harmful effects of alcohol abuse, a sudden religious experience, or the knowledge that one had previously overcome a different problem by self-control. Having made the decision and having started to resolve their drinking problems, it would have been easy to falter. Continuing or maintaining the effort becomes the important consideration once the initial move has been made. Tuchfeld identified social factors as being important in the maintenance of change. It helped if the individual engaged in non-alcohol-related leisure activities, while a stable social and economic background together with encouragement from others were also of

major importance. Overall, many social and psychological factors were found to be implicated in the cessation
of excessive drinking and the maintenance of those
changes. These factors interacted with one another, but
no single factor alone was sufficient to bring about the
resolution of drinking problems. In view of this study,
there is reason to doubt the 'spontaneous' nature of spontaneous remission. The changes did not come about
through formal treatment, but the factors involved in
including and maintaining those changes were ident-
ifiable. Interesting as these results are, the methodology of
the study was such that Tuchfeld expressed appropriate
reservations over their full acceptance. The subjects were
all volunteers, many of whom participated in the study in
response to solicitations in the mass media. It is therefore
not known to what extent the findings of this study apply
to the alcoholics who did not volunteer to participate.
There is evidence that 'volunteers', in general, do differ
in some respects from 'non-volunteers'. The educational
background of the average subject was relatively good,
while four-fifths were urban dwellers. Finally, the data for
the study were obtained from the alcoholics during an
intensive interview. Since no supporting evidence was
sought from other sources, the validity of the results rests
squarely on the memory and honesty of the interviewees.
These difficulties are mentioned not to denigrate the
study, but to remind the reader that flawless studies are
probably impossible, and that judgement has to be exercised over the strengths and weaknesses of studies and,
hence, their findings.

One element in Emrick's (1975) review of psychologically orientated treatments involved comparing the
effectiveness of treatment and no (formal) treatment.
Initially, he compared the outcomes from two groups of
studies. In all cases these outcomes were measured after
a follow-up of six months or more. One group of studies
concerned alcoholics who had received no formal treatment. The other group of studies involved alcoholics who

had received only a minimal amount of formal treatment. Comparison of the outcome data from these two groups revealed no significant differences, so the results from all the studies were pooled together. Finally, the pooled outcome results were compared with abstinent and 'total-improved' rates in alcoholics whose outcomes were assessed not less than six months after the termination of formal treatment. Statistical analysis revealed that nearly 14 per cent of alcoholics who received no treatment or only minimal treatment were abstinent at six (or more) months follow-up. Twice that figure, 28 per cent of those who received more than minimal treatment, were similarly abstinent. Thus, treatment that is more than minimal results in a larger percentage of abstinent alcoholics than does minimal treatment or no treatment at all. When the data concerning all degrees of improvement are compared, almost 42 per cent of the combined no treatment and minimal treatment alcoholics were improved, against 63 per cent of the more than minimally treated individuals. Overall, these results show that some alcoholics do become abstinent despite receiving no treatment or only a minimal amount of formal treatment, while over two-fifths achieved some degree of improvement. More than a minimal amount of formal treatment results in significantly more abstinent and more improved alcoholics. As Emrick commented, it is good to see that many alcoholics do improve without formal treatment since only a small percentage of them receive treatment for their alcoholism. On the other hand, treatment agencies can take heart in the knowledge that treatment, in general, does help more alcoholics improve than would be the case in the absence of treatment.

Denial and detection

The stereotype of an alcoholic includes the concept of 'denial'. Active alcoholics are said to deny that they have drinking problems, despite being repeatedly confronted with evidence of that problem. Denial has at least two aspects, which I shall refer to as 'conscious', and 'unconscious' denial, respectively. Conscious denial implies that the individual is aware, however dimly, that his or her drinking is problematic. This type of denial involves a conscious attempt to deceive others, and maybe oneself, about the seriousness and extent of one's problem. It may be expressed in affronted 'hurt', 'misunderstood', exasperated, even humorous terms. The common denominator is that the alcoholic is at least partially, and perhaps fully, aware that a problem does exist. 'Covering up' is a frequent topic of conversation among some alcoholics; for example, members of Alcoholics Anonymous. A brief acquaintance with members of that fellowship will convince one that there are more ways of concealing bottles than one would have dreamed possible. This behaviour is part of the wider concern about keeping the existence or extent of the drinking problem to oneself. Unconscious denial is a different matter since it involves denial of the facts but with no desire to deceive. This type of denial is directed towards oneself. Thus, an actively drinking alcoholic may be oblivious to the personal and interpersonal harm resulting from excessive drinking, or may lay the blame on something other than alcohol. Such a person may indignantly deny there is anything wrong, if pressed to acknowledge his or her drinking problems. Unconscious denial involves deception of oneself, in the first place, and deception of others in the second. It may be that usually both types of denial are present, although the salience of either may vary with circumstances (Paredes, 1974).

So far, denial on the part of the alcoholic has been considered; denial of the alcoholic's drinking problems by other family members was also discussed in chapter 7. There is no doubt that only a minority of alcoholics do seek treatment. Denial by alcoholics is one contributory factor but other factors also operate. There is evidence that physicians frequently fail to identify the alcoholics among their patients. Any general practitioner's list of 2,000 patients may well include 20 alcoholics. It is surprising that many general practitioners will claim to have only 'one or two' alcoholics on their list. There is also evidence that physicians often fail to ask patients about their drinking (Ruprecht 1970). One reason for this failure to detect or diagnose alcoholism is that medical education has paid insufficient attention to this problem. Physicians have not been equipped with the knowledge that would enable them to suspect and diagnose alcoholism. Further reasons for this diagnostic failure have also been suggested. Lisansky (1974) pointed out that most physicians come from middle-class, professional backgrounds that foster and value moderation, self-control and personal responsibility. These values are also applied to drinking. Excessive drinking is viewed with distaste and the (immoderate, uncontrolled, irresponsible) alcoholic is regarded as a pathetic figure. All this results in the physician having a 'blind spot' for alcoholism. Additional factors may also operate. Alcoholics have a reputation for being 'bad' patients. Their word is unreliable, they fail to comply with the treatment regimen prescribed by the doctor, they upset other patients, and they do not respond to treatment. Physicians, like most people, do not relish failure and so may avoid treating the 'untreatable' alcoholics. This brings us full circle, since a failure to diagnose and treat may result from denial.

There are solutions to the problems of denial and diagnostic failure on the part of some alcoholics and therapists. If both groups ceased to construe drinking problems as shameful and something that should be concealed, then the emotional 'loading' would disappear and denial becomes unnecessary. This change in attitudes is most likely to come about through education of the public and those professionals who deal with alcoholics. Improved diagnostic skills can be taught, and various attempts are being made to make detection more likely. Wilkins's (1974) book, *The Hidden Alcoholic in General Practice*, describes the results of just such an attempt.

A burgeoning area, particularly in North America, is that of treatment programmes for alcoholic employees. Trades unions, employers, employers' organizations and voluntary associations have individually and co-operatively established about 3,000 programmes for alcoholic employees. Some measures of the importance of this movement can be gained from the fact that there are over 2,000 members of the Association of Labor and Management Administrators and Consultants on Alcoholism (ALMACA), while the National Council on Alcoholism publishes a specialized journal, the *Labor Management Journal on Alcoholism*. In the United Kingdom, the Health and Safety Executive, the Health Departments, and the Department of Employment jointly published a paper: The Problem Drinker at Work (1981). The declared purpose of that document was to provide guidance: '. . . on ways in which employers and trade unions can assist the Health Service and Health Departments in their programmes for people with drinking problems' (p.1.). This is a welcome move and one that, hopefully, will bear fruit. Although there are no signs of a rush to establish alcoholism programmes, it is important that those wishing to do so should take heed of the results obtained and the problems encountered in North America (Roman 1981).

Numerous indicators could be mentioned supporting the general conclusion that there is a growing awareness, among the public, employers, trade unions and health care professionals and the government, of the nature and seriousness of drinking problems. However, awareness alone is unlikely to encourage problem drinkers to seek treatment, and professionals to offer treatment, unless effective treatments and acceptable treatment goals are available. It is to the issue of treatment goals that I now turn.

Treatment goals

There can be no doubt that the most widely accepted goal of treatment is abstinence. Abstinence is the goal of Alcoholics Anonymous, as it is and has been of most treatment agencies. It is simple enough to see how this came about. The concept of lifelong abstinence is widely understood, and easily defined as the complete and uninterrupted absence of any alcohol intake. Given valid information about the individual's drinking status, it is easy to decide whether he or she is abstinent. Any intake of alcohol means that the individual concerned is not abstinent. Aside from the apparent clarity and simplicity of the abstinence goal, there is probably an even more influential reason for adopting that treatment goal. Alcoholism is difficult to treat and, typically, therapeutic progress is punctuated with relapses into excessive drinking. If the therapist's theoretical model of alcoholism includes the loss of control hypothesis, then the inability to drink alcohol in moderation is a defining characteristic of alcoholism. Only the abstinent alcoholic is 'cured'. It follows that abstinence must be that therapist's treatment goal for his or her patient. Anything less indicates treatment failure. This is most clearly observable in the lifelong abstinence goal of Alcoholics Anonymous. Given the vehement adherence by members of that fellowship to the loss of control hypothesis, abstinence is the only conceivable goal. Pervasive as this treatment goal is, it is increasingly being challenged by empirical studies.

There is strong evidence that some alcoholics who have undergone abstinence-oriented treatments eventually return to 'normal', non-harmful drinking (e.g. Davies

1962; Kendell 1968; Lemere 1953). A familiar objection to this finding is that the individuals concerned were not 'real' or 'genuine' alcoholics. The basis of this claim appears to be the view that the 'alcoholic' who returns to normal drinking cannot, by definition, have been a 'real' alcoholic in the first instance. It is extremely unlikely that this claim of misdiagnosis could possibly account for all the cases that have been reported of resumed normal drinking. A second concern about abstinence as the sole treatment goal arises from evidence regarding the general adjustment of abstinent alcoholics. Gerard, Saenger and Wile (1962) found that a large proportion of the alcoholics in their study showed poor adjustment and were perceptibly disturbed, despite having achieved abstinence. A third reason against uncritically accepting abstinence as the only worthwhile therapeutic goal comes from the recent work on controlled drinking. There is ample evidence that some alcoholics do resume normal drinking after undergoing therapy whose declared goal is 'controlled drinking' (Sobell and Sobell 1973a, b, 1976).

In his review of 265 psychologically oriented treatment studies, Emrick (1974) found a one-third abstinence rate and a one-third additional 'improvement' rate. Overall, there is abundant evidence that, for whatever reasons, lifelong abstinence is not adopted by the majority of treated patients. This fact alone raises the question of whether abstinence is the 'best' goal for the majority of alcoholics.

In recent years the therapeutic goal of 'controlled drinking' has become a matter of heated debate among therapists who treat alcoholics. There are two schools of thought on the subject. There are those who believe that lifelong abstinence is the only therapeutic goal that should be entertained. The proponents of this view are usually strong in their condemnation of any attempt to teach controlled (problem-free) drinking, regarding such attempts as misguided and, in terms of the alcoholic's long-term welfare, dangerous. The other school of thought holds that controlled drinking is an appropriate and realistic goal for some alcoholics. Both camps cite evidence in support of their own position, sometimes drawing different conclusions from one and the same study. This becomes possible when there is no mutually, or generally, agreed criteria by which to judge the 'successfulness' of therapy. A single example will make this clear. Ewing and Rouse (1976) attempted to inculcate controlled drinking in alcoholics. The treatment method used was similar to that used by Sobell and Sobell (1973a) but it 'failed' in Ewing and Rouse's case. While Sobell and Sobell continue to maintain the view that some alcoholics can learn to drink in a controlled, non-harmful, manner, Ewing and Rouse claimed that their well-conducted study had shown this to be an untenable position. The source of the differing views resides in the criterion for 'success'. Sobell and Sobell (1973a) broadly define their success criteria in such a way that, against a general background of controlled drinking, an occasional uncontrolled drinking episode does not signify therapeutic failure. It is regarded as an unfortunate occurrence but not as a disaster. Thus, the Sobells' outcome criteria involve degrees of 'improvement'. They do not expect their controlled-drinking programme to produce totally controlled drinking. Ewing and Rouse (1976) set their criterion of success as totally controlled drinking, and criterion of failure as one or more episodes of uncontrolled drinking. According to these criteria, the programme did fail. Notice that if these maximally stringent criteria were applied to the Sobells' study, that too would be regarded by Ewing and Rouse as a failure.

The difficulty that arises from using success criteria that preclude any deviation from 'perfection' is that few human endeavours could then be construed as 'successful'. Even the best typists make typing errors, but they are not then regarded as 'failures'. If the only criterion for being a successful physician was that of keeping one's patients alive, then most, if not all, physicians would be deemed to have failed at some time. Returning to the subject of controlled drinking, there is ample evidence that considerable 'improvements' can be achieved by those who undergo suitable training in controlled drinking (e.g. Lloyd and Salzberg 1975; Miller and Caddy 1977). One frequent objection to this goal is that it entails too great a risk of the alcoholic sliding into uncontrolled drinking. Research over the last two decades indicates that this need not be the outcome. I agree with those who believe that the real therapeutic problem is one of identifying those alcoholics for whom abstinence is the 'best' goal, and those for whom controlled drinking is to be preferred (Miller and Caddy 1977; Pattison 1976).

Before leaving the important matter of therapeutic goals, it is necessary to consider one that goes beyond abstinence and drinking. It has already been mentioned that abstinence does not, in itself, automatically result in good general life adjustment of the individual (e.g. Pattison 1976). The same is likely to be true of controlled drinking. This has led some workers to advocate the broader goal of 'life health' (Pattison 1976), or improvement in the 'quality of life', (Miller and Foy 1981). Pattison (1976) advocates approaching rehabilitation in terms of five distinct areas of 'life health', including drinking health, emotional health, vocational health, interpersonal health and physical health. This is consonant with the movement in the health care professions to treat the 'whole' person, rather than a single aspect of the individual. According to this view, it is unwise to treat the alcoholic for his or her excessive drinking in the expectation that the alcohol-related problems will correct themselves. Pattison (1976) makes the important point that an alcoholic may not be impaired in each of the five life health areas.

In general, there is a growing awareness that single,

unitary treatment goals are unlikely to be appropriate in cases of alcoholism. Alcoholism typically involves multiple impairments, so multiple goals are necessary. While it is usually unwise to concentrate therapeutic efforts exclusively on drinking, in many cases drinking must be modified, or must cease, before other 'life health' problems can be tackled effectively. For example, poly-neuropathy (peripheral nerve damage), malnutrition, marital and financial problems are unlikely to yield to treatment if the alcoholic is continuously intoxicated.

Treatment by whom?

There is evidence that alcoholics are able to carry out their own 'therapy' without the formal intervention of any second party. This was true of the two co-founders of Alcoholics Anonymous. No data appear to be available on the subject of completely self-devised and directed therapy and, for obvious reasons, a representative sample of such data would be difficult to collect. There has been some interest in recent years in 'minimal' contract therapy. This typically takes the form of an initial assess-ment interview, the handing out of a printed treatment booklet and subsequent telephone follow-ups. Miller, Gribskov and Mortell (1981) divided self-referred problem drinkers into two groups, one group receiving minimal contact therapy, the other undergoing therapist-directed treatment. At the end of the 10-week treatment period, at least 80 per cent of each group were either abstinent or were drinking significantly less alcohol. These improvements were maintained at three to five-month follow-ups. Interestingly, there were no significant differences between the outcomes of the two groups. These are encouraging results, but as the authors remarked it cannot be assumed that they would have been achieved with a group of alcoholics who had merely bought self-help books. There is an implied difference in the commitment to change between someone who buys a self-help book and someone who actively seeks treatment. That difference could be important. Despite these reservations, the Miller *et al.* (1981) study demonstrates that 'bibliotherapy' with minimal therapist contact can help some alcoholics.

The best known 'self-help' therapy for alcoholics is undoubtedly Alcoholics Anonymous (AA). This organization, or as members prefer to call it, 'fellowship', is run by and for alcoholics. Founded by two abstinent alcoholics in America in 1935, it has spread to many countries and has provided a model for other self-help groups such as Gamblers Anonymous. In Britain, there are more than 1,000 local branches, or chapters, and the number increases yearly. Meetings are held at least once a week, usually more frequently, and members may participate regularly in more than one group. An important feature of AA is that it recognizes the impact of alcoholism on the family and friends of the alcoholic, so Alanon caters for the family and friends, whilst Al-Ateen provides support for the alcoholic's teenage children. The fellowship provides a reasonably comprehensive approach to alcoholism and, in many instances, there is referral between AA and the professional services (such as general practitioners and hospitals). Lifelong abstinence is the only therapeutic goal available. Two additional, major features of the AA approach to alcoholism are the phone-in 'crisis' service, and the visiting team. The former provides a telephone contact service for anyone who has worries about his or her own drinking, or even about someone else's drinking. A wife may telephone wanting to know what she can do about her husband's excessive drinking, for instance. The telephone service also enables abstinent alcoholics who feel in danger of drinking to seek advice and support, in their moment of crisis. While there can be no doubt that AA helps many alcoholics, it appeals to only a minority of the total number of alcoholics. Several studies have indicated that less than one-fifth of alcoholics referred to AA actually attend meetings on a regular basis (Ogborne and Glaser 1981). Possible reasons for this will be discussed later in this chapter.

Many local Councils on Alcoholism have been set up under the auspices of the National Council on Alcoholism. Part of the remit of the local Councils is to set up Alcoholism Information Centres which, despite their title, usually offer counselling to alcoholics and their spouses. Each Alcoholism Information Centre has a director who, typically, fulfils the dual roles of educator and counsellor, although there may be additional counsellors on the staff. The type of counselling provided varies widely, some being based on the AA model, some deriving from social case work practice, and some being of a broadly eclectic nature. Some centres advocate lifelong abstinence as the only realistic goal, whilst others include controlled drinking in a range of options. The precise choice of goals is by agreement between client and counsellor, of course. My own informal impression is that Alcoholism Information Centres provide one alternative source of help for alcoholics who are not attracted to AA. Having said that, I must also point out that some alcoholics patronize both organizations. One important difference between AA and the Alcoholism Information Centre is that the latter can probably more easily accommodate those people who have drinking problems but who do not believe they have reached the parlous state described by many AA members.

Before turning to the statutory providers of treatment, it is important to be clear that there are additonal non-statutory bodies providing rehabilitation to alcoholics. It should not be thought that theirs is an insignificant contribution, since they provide 80 per cent of all community-based services for alcoholics (FARE 1979). Between them those non-statutory organizations have 63 residential facilities in England and Wales. In order to improve communication and co-operation between these organizations, they have formed the Federation of Alcoholic Rehabilitation Establishments (FARE). As one might hope, referrals between the member organizations, other non-statutory bodies, and statutory bodies is commonplace. Thus, the importance of the role played by non-statutory organizations in the rehabilitation of alcoholics should not be underestimated.

General practitioners detect some cases of alcoholism, and usually refer them on to another professional colleague. I suspect that psychiatrists receive the majority of these referrals, although clinical psychologists receive their share either by direct GP referral or from psychiatrists. One major reason why GPs are sometimes reluctant to treat alcoholics is because a busy GP often cannot find the time to undertake what tends to be a time-consuming treatment regimen.

There may be a considerable overlap between the types of treatments provided by psychiatrists, clinical psychologists and social workers. The psychiatrist is the only one of this trio who is able to prescribe drugs and who has in-patient beds in a hospital. Detoxification units are usually headed by a psychiatrist, since the avoidance and amelioration of withdrawal symptoms may require medical expertise. Likewise, the physical condition of the alcoholic may have deteriorated, necessitating a medical intervention. Social workers may have a special part to play through their access to a variety of statutory agencies, and their practice of visiting their clients at home. The clinical psychologist's special contribution is that of assessing the course of treatment, the immediate and long-term outcomes. If the three professionals shared the same therapeutic approach to alcoholism, apart from their special contributions, the ways in which they would independently handle the same case would be similar.

It has already been pointed out that alcoholism is a

multifaceted problem. It is probably unreasonable to expect one professional or one individual to have all the knowledge, skills and contacts necessary to conduct a multifaceted therapeutic or 'rehabilitation' programme. This simple fact has led to the concept of the multidisciplinary therapeutic team; an approach that is well established in treatment and rehabilitation following problems such as limb amputation, stroke, heart attack, multiple injuries occasioned by transport accidents, and so forth. Although there is general agreement that a multidisciplinary team approach is, theoretically, ideal, it is difficult to achieve in practice. The reasons for this are complex and will not be considered except at a superficial level. Suffice it to say that interprofessional demarcation disputes over clinical and medical responsibilities, traditional practices, hierarchical power structures, and so forth, all conspire to make multidisciplinary co-operation more problematic than one would wish it to be. However desirable they may be, genuine multidisciplinary team approaches to alcoholism are rare indeed (Krasner 1977).

Treatment where?

The generally held view is that, unless there are good reasons for adopting a different course, patients should be treated in the community. This applies to the treatment of the broad range of ills suffered by human beings. As a general rule, it is assumed that, for most patients, hospitals and similar institutions are the preferred treatment locations only when community-based interventions are proscribed. Many reasons are offered in support of this view, including the notion that patients respond best on non-alien environments; hospitals, according to this view, being 'alien'. They are alien in the sense that they are unfamiliar, possibly intimidating, they can be impersonal, and so on. The patient's natural environment, the community, is usually assumed to be benign. Clearly, some conditions require hospital treatment, as is the case with most surgical procedures, although early discharge back into the community is the rule, nowadays. Thinking also changes, as in the matter of childbirth. Fifty years ago, home deliveries were the norm. During the last decade or two hospital confinements were advocated. The wheel seems to be going full circle, because increasing numbers of women are opting for home deliveries. It will be clear to the reader that these trends are not arbitrary, but are in response to changes in medical and public thinking and convenience. Aside from in-patient treatment, many conditions are treated on an outpatient basis, but the point of therapeutic contact is still the hospital.

The majority of alcoholics are treated in the community by AA, Alcoholism Information Centres, non-statutory residential facilities and general practitioners, to name only the most obvious ones. Hospital outpatient treatment is also common. The general philosophy behind this approach is that since alcoholism is multifaceted, occurring within a community setting, and as its ramifications extend into the alcoholic's community, the patient is best treated in the community. The alternative is to carry out in-patient treatment in a hospital or, where available, in an alcoholism unit attached to a hospital. In-patient treatment is necessary in certain cases. The process of reducing an alcoholic's habitual high blood alcohol concentration to a low, usually a zero, level, is formally known as 'detoxification' and informally as 'drying out'. If withdrawal symptoms, with the possibility of delirium tremens and epileptic convulsions are to be avoided, it may be necessary to keep the individual under close observation and to provide suitable medication. It is sometimes necessary to carry out in-patient treatment when, as is frequently the case, the alcoholic's immediate community actively supports and encourages his or her excessive drinking. In-patient treatment provides a separation from the drinking environment and is usually a necessary prerequisite for successful recovery. This illustrates why community-based treatment is unlikely to be best for all alcoholics. Ultimately, in-patient treatment ends and is usually followed by out-patient or community-based treatment. In some cases, this change from one type of treatment and from one treatment location to another, presents a stumbling block. One way of avoiding this transition would be to carry out all treatment in the community, but, as we have seen, this may currently be impossible and undesirable. Another solution to the transition problem is to make it less abrupt, but introducing an intermediate stage. 'Halfway houses' provide a 'sheltered' community residence in which, and from which, patients can begin to re-establish themselves in the community at large. The majority of these houses in Great Britain are run by non-statutory organizations, many or whom are members of FARE (Federation of Alcoholic Rehabilitation Establishments), as mentioned earlier. 'Day Centres', typically run by non-statutory bodies, provide yet another transitional stepping-stone for some alcoholics and, in some instances, probably represent the only source of help sought by the alcoholic. Day centres vary in the facilities they provide, although these may include leisure activities, refreshments, and counselling sessions if requested. One feature of most Day Centres is that they are often located in town centres for easy access, so that clients may drop in as often and for as long as they wish. The reader will recognize that Day Centres and Alcoholism Information Centres provide two community-based sources of help for alcoholics, and routes through which they may be referred to the statutory organizations. Both potentially cater for the full range of alcoholics, but another type of urban facility is particularly aimed at the homeless or vagrant alcoholic. 'Shop Fronts' have been set up in a number of urban areas to provide homeless and vagrant alcoholics with a 'door' by which to gain access to the statutory and non-statutory services. As their name indicates, a Shop Front is an ordinary high street shop that has been taken over to provide a particular service. The staff provides information and advice to anyone who drops in, besides assessing the suitability of clients for referral. An essential feature is that no commitment to enter treatment is required of those who use the Shop Front. Some clients may never proceed beyond the occasional brief visit, although others may grasp the nettle and agree to be referred on for treatment. Shop Fronts are contact points, assessment and referral agencies; they are not treatment facilities.

Chapter 10

Treatments

There are so many approaches to the treatment of alcoholism that it would require a book many times the size of this one to provide an adequate account of them all. My purpose, here, is to identify and sketch out some treatment types so that the reader will appreciate the diversity of the available methods. A more detailed account would go beyond the scope of this book, so the interested reader could start by seeking out some of the references provided in the remainder of this chapter.

Abstinence-oriented treatments

Pharmacological

One way of ensuring that an abstinent alcoholic does not drink alcohol is by means of chemical control. The patient takes a tablet every day and suffers no adverse effects unless alcohol is consumed. If alcohol is taken, a variety of highly unpleasant symptoms are induced, including flushing, sweating, nausea and giddiness, as well as a general feeling of being acutely unwell. These effects are so unpleasant that it is usual to demonstrate them to the individual before allowing him or her to begin this treatment. One reason for this is that individual responses differ and can, in some cases, lead to shock and even death. Two drugs are in common use: Antabuse and Absten. The latter, newer drug is sometimes preferred because it tends to have fewer side-effects than the former. The fact is that alternatives are available. The obvious difficulty is that this treatment completely relies on the patient strictly adhering to the prescribed drug regimen. A related point is that if the chemical control is lifted, or if the drug is withdrawn, there is nothing to prevent the alcoholic from resuming drinking. Finally, the treatment is not without risks, and can only be prescribed for patients who wish to remain abstinent and are not careless of their own well-being. For these reasons, chemical control is not suitable as the sole treatment. It can be helpful in the earlier stages of a treatment programme which requires abstinence in the short, medium or long term. Some patients, while anxious to remain abstinent, doubt their ability to do so. Chemical assistance is often welcome in such cases.

Advice

There has been a largely unchallenged assumption in the past that longer duration and higher intensity treatments result in better patient outcomes than short duration, low-intensity ones. There is some evidence that this is not always the case. Edwards *et al.* (1977) conducted a controlled trial of 'treatment' and 'advice'. The purpose of the study was to compare the outcomes from, on the one hand, a therapeutic package of the sort that an alcoholic would be likely to receive in a well-supported treatment centre and, on the other hand, a single, brief minimal advice session. As the authors commented, the single consultation advice session, received by the 'advice' group, would certainly be regarded as inadequate by most therapists.

Fifty male alcoholics were randomly assigned to each group. All were told that they were suffering from alcoholism and advised to aim for total abstinence. The 'treatment' group were offered chemical control, drugs to ameliorate withdrawal, an introduction to AA, psychiatric care for the husband and social work support for his wife, and in-patient care if necessary. The treatment programme was flexible and gradually changed from being a high- to being a low-intensity intervention. In contrast, after the initial counselling session, the 'advice' group were essentially told that no further appointments would be made for them because achieving and maintaining the goal of abstinence was something only they could do. Progress reports were obtained from both groups at four-weekly intervals. One year after the initial interviews both groups had improved over a broad range of measures but, overall, there was no significant difference between the two groups. Although this study has been the subject of much detailed criticism, my own view is that its findings cannot be dismissed. Taking the more conservative estimates provided by the alcoholics' wives after one year, about one third of the patients in each group had only a 'slight' or 'no' drinking problem. This success rate is well within the mean success rate of the broad range of alcoholism treatments. These results certainly do not mean that only 'advice' or minimal treatment should be provided for alcoholics. It does mean that new treatment methods need to be developed and rigorously tested, while additional emphasis should be placed on prevention. Notice that the results from this study may not generalize to different groups of alcoholics. All the subjects were married and living with their wives. The outcome might be different for divorced or single men. Likewise, although the 'treated' group were apparently involved in a comprehensive treatment package, the conclusions drawn from this study may not apply to other forms of treatment. What the study does show is that, under some circumstances, relatively complex treatments fail to produce better outcomes than minimal treatment. More treatment did not produce better outcomes than less treatment.

Psychoanalysis

Classical psychoanalysis may involve five daily interviews each week, over a period of some years. Even if this form of treatment was shown to be extremely effective in the treatment of alcoholism, there are so few practising psychoanalysts that they could not cope with the number of potential patients. To the best of my knowledge, there has been no adequately controlled demonstration that classical psychoanalysis is an effective treatment for alcoholism. The same lack of demonstrated efficacy applies to the 'brief' psychoanalytic procedures that have been developed in recent years. One major problem with evaluating psychoanalytic approaches is that the criteria for a successful outcome of treatment need not include symptom removal. Thus, according to this view, a successfully treated alcoholic might, nevertheless, continue to drink excessively. Success, in such a case, might be assessed in terms of the extent to which the drinker understands and can come to terms with his or her excessive drinking. There again, it might be assessed in terms of the extent to which a range of intrapsychic conflicts has been resolved. The crucial point is that these criteria are not accessible to objective measurement. Reliance therefore has to be placed in the subjective evaluations of the therapist and patient. The problems become yet more difficult because therapist and patient may disagree about the outcome.

Group approaches that have a broadly psychoanalytic rationale are in fairly common use with in-patient alcoholics, but their contribution is difficult, if not impossible, to assess, since they are always but one part of a larger therapeutic programme.

Transactional analysis

An exception to the last statement is transactional analysis. This variant of psychodynamic group therapy was developed by Berne (1964), and its application to alcoholism was briefly described in the previous chapter. A major aim of the transactional analyst is to bring into the open the nature of the 'game' being played by the alcoholic. Since the prime focus is on interpersonal transactions, the spouse, or other principle 'players' are also involved in treatment. Again, so there shall be no misunderstanding about the use of the technical term 'game', this is not defined as a pleasant and amusing piece of fun, but as a covert, manipulative and destructive battle, in which at least one participant expects to gain an advantage. A further purpose of the transactional analyst is to help the alcoholic, and other principal players, to find, try and develop new non-destructive 'adult' modes of relating.

Many who work with alcoholics do find it useful to conceptualize alcoholism within a transactional analytic framework. More particularly, the purpose and meaning of a particular behavioural episode can sometimes be understood or interpreted through this model in a way that has an immediate intuitive appeal. Criticisms of the fundamental model were provided in the previous chapter, so they will not be repeated here. No adequate controlled studies have yet been reported on the treatment of alcoholism by transactional analysis, but successful single-case studies have been reported.

Behavioural treatments

The behavioural explanation of alcoholism was discussed in the previous chapter, and it was asserted that this model provides the basis for a comprehensive treatment approach. Early behavioural methods drew heavily on laboratory-based animal analogue studies, with the result that simplistic treatments were applied to the complex problem of alcoholism. Although these methods are now unlikely to be used in isolation, one or more may be included in a treatment 'package'. For this reason, and because they were important in the development of more comprehensive and sophisticated behavioural approaches, some of these unidimensional methods will be considered before turning to the more recent multidimensional interventions. A particular feature of behaviour therapy research is the strong emphasis placed on measurement and experimental rigour. Strenuous and painstaking efforts are made to characterize the patients and the treatment they receive. Many aspects of the patients' functioning are assessed before, during and after treatment, so that the efficacy of the treatment can be determined and reported in the most comprehensive and objective way possible. An important consequence is that studies should be replicable and their results directly comparable. In general, scientific rigour and objectivity are highly prized.

Aversion therapies   The purpose of aversion therapy is to make alcohol so aversive to the alcoholic that it is avoided. Classical conditioning is the theoretical mechanism by which the repeated association of an aversive event (e.g. electric shock, nausea, vomiting) with alcohol (sight, smell, taste) results in alcohol becoming aversive. In other words, alcohol becomes repellent. The Romans may have been the first to use aversion therapy to cure alcohol abuse. They would surreptitiously place an eel in the toper's wine cup, the drinker would be aghast and nauseated by what lurked at the bottom. The sight, taste and smell of alcohol was paired with an aversive stimulus.

In electrical aversion therapy the patient receives unpleasant electric shocks, usually to the hands, arms or legs, when alcohol passes the lips and while it is retained. The shocks are terminated when the alcohol is spat out. This procedure is usually repeated 20 to 50 times daily over a period of 10 days or so. Thus, alcohol is associated with unpleasant electric shocks 200 to 500 times. An important part of the procedure is that of having available an alternative response to drinking alcohol. The patient is thereby not prevented from acting, at all, but has the opportunity of consuming a soft drink, or of eating a sweet, for example. Behaviour, as such, is not punished: only drinking alcohol. Although this procedure could be carried out in a consulting room or laboratory, it is often performed in surroundings that are similar to those in which the patient normally drinks. The public house drinker would receive treatment in a simulated bar, the home drinker in a simulated living room. This is an attempt to ensure generalization of the treatment effects to the patient's normal drinking environment. Theoretically, a failure to facilitate generalization could result in alcohol becoming aversive to the patient only in the consulting room or laboratory in which the treatment took place. Generalization and the enhancement of treatment effects has also been promoted by providing patients with their own, small portable shock generators. These are small enough to wear on a belt or to carry in a pocket. The patient is instructed to shock him or herself whenever the thought of drinking occurs, whenever alcohol is purchased, poured out or consumed. This should ensure the most direct and widest possible generalization of the treatment effects. Theoretically, aversion treatments should 'automatically' result in an aversion or indifference towards alcohol. Despite a fairly long history (the first electrical aversion treatment of alcoholism was carried out in Russia by Kantorovich in 1929), the clinical usefulness of this procedure has not been fully resolved. It does appear to be effective with some patients, but it is not clear whether the effective component of treatment is the aversive conditioning itself, or the additional therapeutic components that typically accompany treatment. I have in mind exhortations to avoid places where alcohol is available, and suggestions about alternative responses to situations in which the patient would normally drink. Again, the expectations of success that the patient brings to treatment, the enthusiasm of the therapist, and the impression that the procedure makes upon the alcoholic, may all be important contributory factors to success or failure. These issues can only be resolved by well-controlled studies, but an insufficient number of such studies has been reported, to date.

A second type of aversion therapy involves the use of nausea-inducing drugs, and an extensive investigation of this procedure was carried out by Voegtlin and colleagues during the 1940s. The alcoholic patients were given a pint of warm saline solution to drink which also contained an emetic. Next they were injected with a mixture of drugs to produce nausea, vomiting, sweating and salivation. Just before the patients felt nauseous and vomited, they took one ounce of whisky into their mouths but did not swallow it. Thus, the taste, smell and effects on the mouth and tongue of the alcohol were followed by intense nausea and vomiting. Each 45-minute session involved two or three trials (saline, injection, alcohol, nausea and vomiting), an average of four to six sessions being run on alternate days, over about 10 days. Following treatment, 'booster' sessions were run after six and 12 months, although additional boosters were available to patients any time they experienced a strong desire to drink. The treatment typically included additional components, such as psychotherapy, vocational and family counselling, advice, and pharmacological measures, for example. While this represents a broad and comprehensive treatment programme, it is not possible to be certain of the extent to which the chemical aversion procedure contributed to the outcome of therapy. Be that as it may, Voegtlin and Broz (1949), and Lemere and Voegtlin (1950) provided data on more than 4,000 patients over a 13-year follow-up period. Total abstinence was achieved by 57 per cent of the patients over that period. This is only slightly less than the 60 per cent rate after the first year. These are impressive results, but certain reservations should be noted. All patients were fee-paying and voluntary, as well as being socio-economically and vocationally stable. Lemere and Voegtlin (1950) commented that chemical aversion therapy may be particularly suitable for this type of patient, but unsuitable for socio-economically disadvantaged and unmotivated alcoholics. Subsequent studies by other investigators have yielded abstinence rates in the range 30 to 80 per cent.

It is difficult to evaluate the direct effects of electrical and chemical aversion therapies because those procedures have been used typically as part of a larger treatment programme. One theoretical advantage of the electrical procedures is that the timing of the shock can be managed precisely, whereas there is a larger margin of error and a greater need for patient co-operation with the chemical method. Conversely, the available evidence favours the chemical procedure. High quality, well-controlled research is required to determine the part that electrical and chemical aversion therapies have to play in the treatment of alcoholism.

Cautela (1970) has developed an aversion therapy that relies only on speech and imagery. Chemical and electrical procedures involve associating nausea and pain, respectively, with the sight, smell and taste of alcohol. Eventually, the sight, smell and taste of alcohol are expected to become aversive to the alcoholic. The emphasis in covert sensitization is on the behaviours and thoughts that preceded drinking alcohol, although drinking is also included. In a typical treatment session, the patient relaxes and, usually, closes his or her eyes. The therapist instructs the patient to become as deeply engrossed as possible in the scene that is about to be described. The therapist might proceed, as follows, adding and elaborating to achieve the most potent aversive image. I shall assume the patient is male. Imagine it is a warm summer day and you are picnicking in a local park with your wife and children. You are all having a marvellous time and you have never felt closer to your family. You have been playing with the children but now you have stopped for some refreshment. You watch your wife pouring out drinks for everyone, but you are thinking about the can of beer that you slipped into the bag. As you do so, you feel a bit sick and begin sweating profusely. You decide that a drink will put things right so you reach into the bag for the can. You are now feeling nauseous and you feel your stomach lurching. You knock over the bag and scrabble for the can, hardly noticing that your wife and children are looking at you oddly. You want to say something, but know that you will vomit if you do. You rip off the ring pull and the warm beer spurts up all over your front. The smell of beer is just too much and you feel the vomit surging up to burn your throat. Your eyes are watering and you gasp for air as you desperately take a mouthful of the warm liquid. You think it will be all right now, but as the beer hits your stomach you lose control and spew vomit all over the meal that your wife has laid. Your children scream in terror and cling to your wife as you fall on your hands in the stinking, beery vomit that is soaking into the sand-wiches and cakes. You have no control as you retch and vomit, your only concern being to breathe and survive. You are aware that one or two people have come over to see what the trouble is but you can see they are revolted by the sight of your wallowing in your own vomit. Eventually, your stomach is empty and you are no longer retching. You wipe your hands on the grass and try to clean up with your handkerchief. You can't smell the beer now, and you begin to feel better. Your children are less upset now and your wife suggests you go and clean up with a kitchen roll she is offering you. You take it and start to walk away but then notice the beer can. You feel a surge of nausea, again, but you snatch it up and fling it into a waste bin. You begin to feel better, already, as you walk away and smell the clean fresh air. You buy a bottle of soda water to settle your stomach, using the remainder to wash off the last of the vomit. You become aware of your surroundings again, and the whole episode seems like a bad dream. You feel you never want to drink alcohol again, and this produces a surge of joy.

In practice, this detailed scene is described as vividly as possible, allowing time for the patient to generate the corresponding imagery. The time taken from beginning to end may be between five and 30 minutes, although much depends upon how inventive the therapist is and how well the patient responds. Having undergone this covert sensitization procedure in the therapist's office, the patient is urged to use this imaginal technique in everyday life. Thoughts of drinking, of buying and drinking alcohol are to be repelled by pairing them with aversive imagery. This provides the alcoholic with a 'self-control' procedure that is independent of the therapist, and can be developed by the patient. Therapy may last for several weeks or months, with each treatment session comprising several covert sensitization trials.

There is evidence that this therapeutic method can be effective. Ashen and Donner (1968) compared the outcomes from three groups of alcoholics. One group received nine covert sensitization sessions over three weeks, the second group received a reversed procedure in which the aversive imagery (vomiting and making a mess) preceded imagined drinking, the third group received no treatment at all. It was observed during treatment that the responses of the second group matched those of the first, so the two were combined. The combined treatment group was instructed to use covert sensitization as a self-control procedure, and they were taught a method of physical relaxation. At six-month follow-up, the patient and one relative completed separate questionnaires about the alcoholic's drinking history after treatment. The no-treatment 'control' patients were all drinking excessively. In contrast, 40 per cent of the treated patients were abstinent at follow-up. These are encouraging results, although the contributions of the therapist-directed part of the treatment, the patient's self-control procedure, and the relaxation training cannot be unravelled. This type of aversion therapy is particularly attractive because it carries no health risks, it is less unpleasant than its chemical and electrical counterparts, it can be used by the patient anywhere and at any time, and it places responsibility for implementing and making the best use of treatment on the patient.

Operant methods The fundamental idea underlying operant conditioning theory is that behaviour is determined by its consequences. Applying this to drinking alcohol, it follows that whether an individual drinks, or remains abstinent, depends upon the consequences. The extent to which someone drinks, the type of beverage consumed, the location of that drinking, the duration of a drinking session, whether drinking is in the company of others or in isolation, all these things are believed to be determined by their consequences. Anything that *increases* the likelihood of a particular behaviour occurring, or encourages the repetition and maintains that behaviour, is known technically as a 'positive reinforcer' or, more often, as a 'reinforcer'. Conversely, anything that *reduces* the likelihood of a particular behaviour occurring, or discourages the repetition and maintenance of that behaviour, is known technically as an 'aversive reinforcer' or 'punisher'. There are some common characteristics of reinforcers which one should know about. An event that is reinforcing to one person may be punishing for another. The marathon runner may greatly enjoy running, whereas the same activity may be painfully distressing if undertaken by an untrained non-runner. One kind of music may be highly reinforcing for one individual, but aversive to another. Hence, what is and is not reinforcing varies between people. Having pointed out the idiosyncratic nature of reinforcers, it must be admitted that there are some events that are reinforcers for most people. Friendly company and kind words are valued reinforcers for almost everyone. Food and drink are reinforcers for most hungry people, as are shelter and warmth during cold weather.

A second general characteristic of reinforcers is that they can, under some circumstances, lose their reinforcing properties. They cease to act as reinforcers.

Eating one ice-cream may be highly reinforcing on a hot day, but eating several dozens is unlikely to be. From my own experience I can predict that one ice-cream is fine but a second would be aversive if eaten immediately after the first. As a consequence of eating the first, I am satiated with respect to ice-cream, so ice-cream temporarily ceases to act as a reinforcer.

Operant-conditioning theory has been intensively researched, giving rise to an immense empirical literature that is based on animal and human studies. The account provided here is concerned only with the most basic principles. In principle, modern operant theory is sophisticated enough to be applied to most, if not all, human behaviours. I now turn to ways in which operant theory has been applied to the treatment of alcoholism.

Several in-patient studies have shown that drinking by alcoholics can be brought under contingency control. Drinking in hospital has been shown to depend upon the consequences arising from that drinking. For example, Bigelow *et al.* (1972) gave 19 male, volunteer in-patient alcoholics free access to 95° proof alcohol. However, access to an 'enriched' environment was contingent upon consuming no more than 5 ounces of alcohol per day. The consequence of drinking more than the prescribed limit was that the patient had to remain in his almost bare room, isolated from other patients and the staff, with access only to pureed food. The limit could be observed either by drinking moderately, or by abstinence. Results showed that the contingencies were effective, with excessive drinking occurring during only about 10 per cent of the time. The result of most interest in the present context was that the patients chose to abstain for about 14 per cent of the time. During these periods of abstinence, access to the enriched (pleasant) environment was so reinforcing that abstinence was chosen rather than moderate drinking. Maybe those alcoholics simply preferred not to risk overstepping the drinking limit and, hence, being banished to their rooms. Bigelow and

Liebson (1972) carried out a study with two male in-patient, Skid Row alcoholics. Alcohol could be earned by pressing a lever, a predetermined number of lever presses being required before the drinks were dispensed. It was found that the level of drinking decreased as the number of lever presses required to obtain the alcohol increased. An average of 16 drinks (16 ounces of 95° proof alcohol) per day were consumed when no more than 1,000 lever presses were required to obtain one drink. When 3,000 presses were necessary, consumption fell to about half. Finally, at the highest work rate, of 5,000 lever presses per drink, the two patients chose to remain abstinent.

It can be seen from the previous examples that the drinking of an in-patient alcoholic can be modified by simple procedures. Money, continuing access to alcohol, weekend leaves and so forth, can be made contingent upon the alcoholic drinking below a stated level. If it is arranged that alcohol is available contingent upon no more than a moderate amount of work by the patient, he or she will continue to drink. If a great deal of work is required to obtain a small amount of alcohol, there comes a point beyond which drinking ceases. Colloquially, one might say that the amount of alcohol obtained does not make the effort worthwhile. More formally, one would say that the 'response cost' is too high. The alert reader will recognize that this is an example of a former rein-forcer (alcohol) failing to act as a reinforcer. Under the contingencies determined by the experimenter, alcohol loses its reinforcing properties. If alcohol was suddenly made freely available to that alcoholic, drinking would very probably occur.

Although there is no doubt that operant procedures can be used to control in-patient drinking, even to the extent of abstinence, this is difficult to achieve in the alcoholic's natural environment. Even when good contin-gency control has been achieved in hospital, it typically breaks down when the patient returns home. The natural everyday environment is much less controllable than the hospital environment. The hospital 'protects' the alcoholic from the stresses of the outside world, and largely takes control of the patient's life. In the outside world, the patient is unprotected and exposed. Therefore, attempts at arranging reinforcement contingencies in the natural environment need to be broadly based and heroic. This has been achieved and impressive results have been obtained, but at the expense of great organizational effort.

Hunt and Azrin (1973) adopted an operant methodology in their 'community-reinforcement' approach to alcoholism. Space constraints do not allow a detailed account of this broad and complex package here, but even the sketch that follows provides some idea of the lengths that one may have to go to if excellent results are to be obtained. The objectives of the community-reinforcement were, first, to assist the patient to achieve satisfactory vocational, family, marital and social functioning.

In this context, 'satisfactory' functioning signifies that engagement in these areas was reinforcing to the patient. Second, family, marital, social and even vocational situations are reinforcing when they involve pleasant (reinforcing) interactions with others. In the absence of these interpersonal interactions, much of their reinforcing power disappears. This fact was used in treatment. To withhold reinforcement is to institute 'time-out from reinforcement' or 'time-out'. Since the drinking goal of the community-reinforcement approach was abstinence, drinking by the alcoholic resulted in time-out: in reinforcement being witheld. In summary, reinforcement in the four areas of functioning was contingent on abstinence on the part of the subjects. Drinking resulted in time-out from reinforcement until abstinence was, once again, established.

The 16 subjects were divided into two groups of equal size, both groups receiving the same 'standard' hospital care. Although the community-reinforcement group participated in the therapeutic procedure, described below, the other 'control' group did not and no provision was made to provide treatment beyond the 'standard' hospital care. Clearly, the 'control' group is important since its 'controls' for extra-therapeutic factors that are assumed to influence both groups. For example, factors such as spontaneous remission of drinking problems, visits to one's doctor, being out and about in the community, attending sports and social functions, and so forth, might influence all the patients' progress after discharge from hospital. In the absence of a control group one can only draw relatively weak or tentative conclusions about what determined the outcome of treatment. 'Controlled' studies provide stronger evidence.

The community-reinforcement group had access to four areas of counselling. Those without jobs were helped to find employment, the counsellor coaching patients in how to behave in job interviews, escorting them to interviews, taking them to their new employment on the first day, arranging transportation and so forth. Once the patient had acquired a satisfactory job, he was discharged from hospital. Marital counselling was provided for the five married patients and their wives, so that improvements could be achieved in this key area. A variety of marital topics were considered, for instance including financial arrangements, family relations, children, sexual problems, social life and grooming. Single patients living in their parental home were counselled with their parents to provide reciprocal benefits, as in the case of married couples. The parental response to drinking by their son was time-out. In the case of patients who had neither a marital nor a parental family, a foster or 'synthetic' family was sought. Synthetic families comprised people who had reasons to maintain regular contacts with the patient; for example, relatives, a minister of religion, or an employer. The synthetic families were urged regularly to invite the patient for dinner, and to expect him to help out in appropriate ways. Access to the synthetic family was contingent on abstinence. Hunt and Azrin recognized that alcoholics almost invariably have a very small number of friends, all or most of whom have serious drinking problems. The goal of social counselling was to restore and expand the alcoholic's social horizons, at the same time making them contingent on abstinence from alcohol. Drinking was to result in time-out from social interactions; the other party refusing to socialize if the patient drank. One major innovation was the setting up of a self-supporting social club for all the patients, including those who were not in the community-reinforcement group. The club supported a wide range of social activities, but alcohol was excluded. Patients were encouraged to bring wives and friends along, and club members with their own transport gave 'lifts' to those without. Finally, as an added inducement to attend, the patients were given free membership for the first month, after which they had to pay their own dues. The last area of counselling concerned the general availability of reinforcers. The ease with which social contacts can be maintained depends, to some extent, on having a telephone and access to transport (the rural area in which the study was conducted had no public transport). Conversation is easier if one has a range of topics for discussion, and these can be increased through reading newspapers, listening to the radio and watching television. Patients were encouraged to obtain these facilities and, in cases of financial difficulty, initial payments were paid on the patient's behalf. Subsequent payments were his responsibility. Maintenance after discharge from hospital involved visits by the counsellor once or twice weekly. Problems that had arisen were discussed and a variety of possible solutions were offered. Information about the patient's drinking behaviour, employment, marital, family and social functioning was also collected. Two visits were made by the counsellor in the second month and, thereafter, once monthly visits were made up to and including the sixth month. Visits to the social club were noted and informal contact was sometimes made with the counsellor.

This complex treatment programme yielded highly gratifying results. The outcome for the community-reinforcement group was significantly better than that of the control group. The community-reinforcement group spent only 14 per cent of the time drinking, compared to 79 per cent for the control group. The community-reinforcement group was unemployed for only 5 per cent of the time, as against 62 per cent for the control. The community-reinforcement group was absent from the marital, parental or synthetic family 16 per cent of the time, in contrast to a figure of 63 per cent for the control group. Finally, the community-reinforcement group was institutionalized for 2 per cent of the time, against 27 per cent for the control patients.

One cannot help but be impressed by the fact that Hunt and Azrin handled what must have been very complex problems of organization and implementation. This was an 'heroic' study. The results are most impressive although, despite the presence of a matched control group, it is not certain whether contingent community-reinforcement for abstinence produced the excellent outcome. Recall that both groups received the same 'standard' hospital treatment package, and that the community-reinforcement programme involved only one group. The difficulty is that this latter group had much more treatment, involving much more contact with the counsellor, than did the control group. It is conceivable that this aspect of the community-reinforcement package may have made a major contribution to that group's outcome. One should bear in mind that this extra contact time involved 'supporting' and encouraging the alcoholic and family, forming and maintaining what was probably a good therapeutic relationship between counsellor and patient, as well as a host of less obvious factors. The precise part played by the contingent community-reinforcement procedure could only be determined by having a control group that received the same amount of therapeutic and informal contact time with the counsellor, as did the community-reinforcement counterpart. The reader may wonder why it matters how the programme works, in view of the fact that, demonstrably, it does work.

In the first place, theoretical advances that lead to a better understanding of alcoholism and of treatment are highly dependent on sound experimental findings. The theoretician must have empirically derived facts to work with. In the second place, by knowing which therapeutic factors were responsible for a particular outcome, the therapist may be able to increase the quantity, quality, acceptability, salience, even 'impact' of those factors. Although certainty is unattainable, a first-class controlled study can keep avoidable uncertainties at bay.

Alcoholics Anonymous

It is probably a fair assumption that, for most people, Alcoholics Anonymous springs to mind when the treatment of alcoholism is mentioned. This organization regards alcoholism as an incurable disease that, unless arrested, is progressive. Given this view of alcoholism, members of Alcoholics Anonymous do not talk about 'cure' but about 'recovery'. The abstinent alcoholic is referred to as a 'recovering' alcoholic. This reminds the individual that he or she can never afford to become complacent about 'recovery', because a single drink of alcohol would, inevitably, result in a complete 'loss of control'. Three consequences of this strict adherence to the disease model will be mentioned, two that are of immediate importance to the alcoholic, and one that has wider implications. First, by cleaving to the disease model certain important benefits accrue to the alcoholic. He or she is said to be suffering from the disease of alcoholism, rather than suffering as a consequence of gluttonous and self-indulgent drinking. If this conceptualization of alcoholism is accepted, the alcoholic deserves sympathy and understanding, rather than condemnation. The traditional view of most diseases is that they are not self-inflicted, and that the person who contracts a disease is a victim of circumstances beyond his or her control. The sugar diabetic is regarded as a blameless victim, for example. The notion of blamelessness is important because it divests the sufferer of responsibility for the affliction. This is a humane consequence, but it can have detrimental effects on treatment attempts. If the alcoholic is a helpless victim, it could be argued that lapses from abstinence into drinking are not the responsibility of that alcoholic. It just 'happened'. If one assumes that the alcoholic is suffering from a 'loss of control' over drinking, it is easy for the sufferer metaphorically to hand over responsibility for treatment to the therapist (Miller 1976). At its most extreme, it could result in the alcoholic making no effort to participate in his or her treatment. Most readers will appreciate that this would be highly inappropriate. It is interesting that modern medical practice makes strenuous attempts to engage patients in their own treatment. The bronchitic is advised not to smoke, the overweight coronary patient is advised to slim down, and the sugar diabetic is responsible for day-to-day self-medicating. Although medical advice is given, the responsibility for some aspects of treatment rests with the patient. Treatment is a co-operative effort, and has a reduced chance of success in the absence of such co-operation between patient and therapist.

A second consequence of adopting the disease model of alcoholism is that the alcoholic is always 'recovering' but has never 'recovered' or been 'cured'. The disease of alcoholism involves permanent 'loss of control' over drinking. A single drink must eventually lead to excessive drinking. As members of the fellowship often express it: 'One drink away from a drunk'! The sufferer, therefore, lives under a Sword of Damocles. Fear of this sort can help keep the alcoholic abstinent but it can also be double-edged. If the alcoholic drinks even a tiny amount of alcohol, and if the loss of control hypothesis is believed, there is then no incentive to stop drinking. There may even be an incentive to continue to the 'inevitable' drunkenness, just to 'get it over with'.

A third, related and wider consequence that stems from construing alcoholism as an incurable disease is that only one treatment goal, that of a lifelong abstinence, is tenable. When such a view is strongly held and vigorously promulgated by an organization as widely respected as Alcoholics Anonymous, the disease *hypothesis* assumes the guise of fact. While unstintingly acknowledging the very considerable achievement of AA in helping many alcoholics to attain abstinence from alcohol, one should be aware that its philosophy and influence on the areas of alcoholism research and treatment may also have less desirable consequences. Tournier (1979) has speculated about three such consequences. First, he pointed out that the therapeutic effectiveness of AA is unknown and is, in principle, unknowable. This comes about because, for instance, the total membership of the fellowship is unknown, precisely because its members are anonymous. Several attempts have been made to assess AA's success rate, but these estimates do not take into account various biassing factors. It is normal practice for treatment studies to include (as 'failures') those individuals who drop out before treatment is completed. This factor is not taken into account in the published studies of AA's effectiveness. Indeed, it would be extremely difficult to do so. Thus, treatment effectiveness studies are based on those who are current members of the fellowship at the time the surveys are carried out. This is bound to inflate the apparent success rate. Those who remain members of AA do so on a voluntary basis; they are self-selected. Again, participation in treatment effectiveness surveys is voluntary, even among those attending meetings, so this provides a yet further 'refined' or biassed sample. A further complicating factor is that the criteria for membership of AA have not been defined. I have suggested in this book that alcoholism results from many interacting factors, and can occur in individuals representing a wide range of personalities. Tournier has noted that, depending on the personality characteristics of the individual, AA may be more or less attractive. The alienated, lonely, but gregarious alcoholic may have much to gain from AA, whereas the fellowship may have little to offer those who do not have these characteristics. A recent review of the literature by Ogborne and Glaser (1981) supports the view that alcoholics who affiliate with Alcoholics Anonymous do differ in several important ways from those who do not.

Tournier's (1979) second point is that AA construes alcoholism in terms of well-established alcohol addiction, and 'powerlessness' over alcohol. This narrow conceptualization is likely to be of little significance to those whose alcoholism is not yet so fully developed. These 'developing' or 'early-stage' alcoholics may not be able to identify with the AA version of the 'typical' alcoholic, and may drift away. There again, it is possible that these embryonic alcoholics may be so frightened by the prospect of reaching the depths plumbed by AA members that they are frightened into seeking alternative treatment. Conversely, despair may result if the message gets across that their current problems are bound to get worse, and that only then will they be 'ready' for AA. In summary, the narrow conceptualization that AA has of alcoholism may deter many alcoholics from seeking help from the fellowship. Third, and finally, Tournier suggested that AA proselytizing has been so influential, that treatment innovations have been eschewed by many research workers and therapists. In particular, controlled drinking research has been roundly and consistently condemned by the fellowship, on the grounds that the only legitimate treatment goal for an 'alcoholic' is abstinence. Careful empirical research has shown that this is not a universal truth. Some alcoholics have been able to return to controlled drinking. No responsible scientist would suggest that, currently, all alcoholics could achieve this goal and, to the best of my knowledge, no such claim has been made or implied. As the reader will see, below, controlled drinking studies have included only carefully selected alcoholics.

In summary, the place of Alcoholics Anonymous as one major approach to the treatment of alcoholism is assured. It is equally certain that other treatments, and alternative treatment goals to total abstinence are now established and will continue to be developed. Unlike the treatment approach of AA, these more recent innovations are both amenable to sound scientific investigation and are being studied. The results, as seen earlier in this chapter and as will be seen below, are encouraging.

Controlled drinking oriented treatments

It has already been pointed out that a small but noteworthy body of clinical studies has shown that some alcoholics have returned to controlled social drinking after having undergone abstinence-oriented treatments. Although such reports appeared throughout the 1950s, it was the paper by Davies (1962) that brought this matter to a head. Davies provided data on seven chronic alcoholics who, having undergone abstinence-oriented in-patient treatment, had thereafter been drinking moderately for seven to 11 years. Indeed, their drinking was so controlled that none had been intoxicated during that follow-up period. The acrimonious furore that greeted the publication of this painstakingly objective and conservative paper is intelligible only against the background of the then current dogma that alcoholics could not, by definition, sustain moderate drinking patterns. 'Loss of control' as a permanent impairment was accepted as a fact. The data reported by Davies threatened this fundamental 'fact'. Over 20 years later, the goal of controlled drinking is still an extremely emotive issue in some quarters.

I shall now briefly review some empirically established facts concerning controlled drinking by former alcoholics. Notice that my use of the adjective 'former' is intentional. A diagnosis of alcoholism is based on the patient's drinking behaviour and some of its immediate consequences (e.g. addiction to alcohol, withdrawal symptoms, etc.). If the individual ceases to drink 'alcoholically', and displays only controlled drinking, and if this moderate drinking behaviour extends over an extended period of time, the diagnosis of alcoholism ceases to be appropriate. Stated more succinctly, the alcoholic is no longer an alcoholic if he or she ceases to drink 'alcoholically', thereafter, drinking moderately and with control. Just to complete the story, I call the alcoholic who has ceased to drink an 'abstinent' alcoholic. It is only if controlled moderate drinking has become the individual's normal pattern that I use the terms 'former alcoholic', 'controlled drinker' or 'social drinker'.

Aversion procedures

It will be recalled that a variety of aversive procedures has been used to induce abstinence in alcoholics, and that these attempts have met with some success. Electrical aversion therapy has also been used to inculcate controlled drinking. Mills *et al.* (1971) carried out a controlled study in which the experimental group of 13 hospitalized, male alcoholics were treated in pairs in a simulated bar-room setting. The patients were told to drink in a socially acceptable manner and, more specifically, to order only mixed drinks, to sip rather than gulp, and to drink no more than three fluid ounces of 86°-proof beverage. If the patient drank according to these instructions, he received no electric shocks. If, on the other hand, he ordered unmixed drinks, or if he gulped rather than sipped, or if he ordered more than the maximum of three ounces, he received a strong and unpleasant electric shock to the fingers. A lower, milder level of shock was given if, having been strongly shocked for ordering an unmixed drink, he then sipped it, or having ordered a mixed drink, he gulped it. The drinking behaviour of the nine patients who underwent at least 14 treatment sessions did change to conform more closely to the target behaviours originally set by Mills *et al*. Unfortunately, the six-week and six-month follow-up results were disappointing. After six weeks, only two patients were drinking in a controlled manner, although three were abstinent. There was a further deterioration at the six-month follow up. At six-week follow up, none of the control group were drinking in a controlled manner, although two were abstinent. Overall, this study demonstrates that the treatment was effective while the patients remained in the hospital, but that their newly learned controlled drinking skills were highly dependent on the aversive contingency that attended any relaxation of that control.

The problem of maintaining therapeutic gains pervades all alcoholism treatments, and will be considered at the end of this chapter.

Blood alcohol concentration discrimination training

The electrical aversion procedure described above was aimed at teaching a particular behavioural style of drinking. Blood Alcohol Concentration (BAC) discrimination training has the more subtle goal of teaching alcoholics to monitor and estimate the concentration of alcohol in their bloodstream. Once the patient has acquired this primary skill, he or she is taught to maintain moderate alcohol concentrations during normal drinking occasions. In essence, the alcoholic is expected to monitor blood alcohol concentration and, subsequently, to use this skill to achieve controlled drinking. The ability to discriminate different blood alcohol concentrations is taught by getting the patient to attend to his or her own idiosyncratic responses to alcohol. These include behavioural elements (such as impaired co-ordination and loquacity), physiological signs (such as perspiring and facial warmth), emotional states (such as calmness, anxiety and happiness) and cognitive factors (such as speeded or slowed thinking). The patient is asked to estimate his or her blood alcohol concentration at intervals while drinking. Breathalyser feedback is provided to improve the accuracy of those estimates. Having become accurate judges, the patients are allowed free access to alcohol and instructed to maintain their blood alcohol concentration within a certain range. Lovibond and Caddy (1970) administered aversive electric shocks to individuals who exceeded a concentration of 0.065 per cent. Silverstein *et al.* (1974) carried out a similar study but, instead of an aversive procedure, they reinforced subjects for maintaining blood alcohol concentrations in the range of 0.07 to 0.09 per cent. Without going into the fine detail of the outcomes, the results showed that alcoholics can learn accurately to estimate their blood alcohol concentrations. It is unfortunate that the follow-up data comprised solely self-reports and information from relatives or friends. The evidence from Silverstein *et al*'s study is that the ability to provide accurate estimates is gradually lost when external (breathalyser) feedback is no longer available. The familiar problem of therapeutic gains not being maintained arises again.

Broad-scope treatment packages

I wish to provide a fairly detailed account of one particular controlled-drinking programme, because it is probably the best conducted and most extensively assessed one yet reported. I refer to the controlled study carried out by Sobell and Sobell at the Patton State Hospital, California.

Sobell and Sobell (1973a) regarded excessive drinking as a maladaptive coping response to stressors in the drinker's life. They also noted that most people approve of moderate drinking. Abstinence is a minority choice and one that, in itself, may act as a stressor for the alcoholic in treatment. Thus, the Sobells constructed a behavioural treatment programme that was adjusted to the particular requirements of each individual patient: the Individualized Behaviour Therapy (IBT) approach. As would be expected of a behavioural intervention, drinking behaviour itself was a major target for modification. Concurrently, alternative, more constructive coping strategies were taught for use in response to those situations and events that, formerly, had led to excessive drinking.

Seventy alcoholic, male, voluntary in-patients were medically screened and each was assigned to one of four groups. There were two non-drinking groups, one an experimental, the other a control group. There were also two controlled drinking groups, again being subdivided into experimentals and controls. Assignment to the controlled drinking goal depended on the patient fulfilling at least three criteria. He had to request the goal, had to have sufficient social support outside the hospital for that type of drinking behaviour, and/or must have been a successful social drinker at some earlier date. Beyond fulfilling at least two of the above criteria, there had to be agreement by a majority of the project staff that controlled drinking appeared to be a reasonable target for the patient in question. Having decided that a patient was a suitable candidate, his assignment to the experimental or control group was random. All 70 patients received a 'conventional hospital treatment' that comprised large therapy groups, AA meetings, medication, physiotherapy and industrial therapy. The two control groups received no additional treatment. In contrast, members of the two experimental groups each received an extra 17 treatment sessions. Emphasis was placed on elucidating the events and situations (the 'setting conditions') that had habitually led to heavy drinking. Patients were then trained in more adaptive, socially acceptable responses to those setting conditions. Additional situations were constructed to provide the patients with opportunities to practise a variety of alternative responses; their ability to differentiate between effective and ineffective responses was thereby enhanced. Drinking took place in either a simulated bar, or living room that had been built in the hospital, depending on the patient's usual drinking situations. In all except three special 'probe' sessions, drinking in ways that were inappropriate to the particular patient's therapeutic goals was punished by electric shocks delivered to the fingers. In practice, controlled drinking patients received shocks for ordering an unmixed drink, for taking large rather than small sips, for ordering more than three drinks per session. These criteria were based on data relating to normal social drinking. Patients whose goal was abstinence received a one-second shock if they ordered any alcoholic beverage, and if they consumed the drink, they were continuously shocked whilst touching the glass.

During the first two sessions, the patients were allowed to get drunk while being videotaped. They were also questioned to discover the setting conditions that had habitually preceded heavy drinking. Detailed information about the programme was provided in the third session, and they were taught socially acceptable ways of resisting social pressure to drink. The fourth and fifth sessions involved replays of the videotapes made during the first and second sessions, respectively. The patient was confronted by an image of himself drunk, both to enhance motivation for change and to provide feedback concerning setting conditions for heavy drinking, for example. During the sixth session, the patient was given an impossible test to complete and informed of his poor performance. This failure experience enabled the therapist and patient to discuss ways in which that failure was handled and how failures, in general, had been handled in the past. In keeping with good ethical practice, the fact of and reason for deceiving the patient in this session was fully explained to him. The 10 consecutive sessions, from seven to 16, concentrated on a careful investigation of the setting conditions for heavy drinking, on inventing a number of potentially adaptive responses to those conditions, on evaluating the probable outcome of enacting each response, and on practising under simulated conditions those alternatives that seemed most likely to be beneficial. The last half-hour of the 16th session was videotaped.

In the case of abstinence-oriented patients who had ordered no drink during two consecutive sessions, a drink was poured and placed in front of the patient at the start of the next session. Drinking resulted in a continuous shock. If the patient decided not to drink, he had to pour the drink down the sink. This 'prompt' to drink was repeated at quarter-hourly intervals throughout the session. The final session included a summary of the patient's progress through the programme, and replaying selected excerpts from the two drunken sessions and the 16th (to emphasize the contrast). Each patient was additionally provided with a card on which various recommendations were printed regarding his treatment and future conduct (a 'Do's and Do not's' card). Finally, the patient was encouraged to apply the self-analysis of his own behaviour, together with alternative response generation and implementation, to all areas of his life. By promoting generalizations of this sort, one would hope that this approach would become a deeply ingrained part of the individual's approach to life.

Almost all the patients were discharged from hospital within a fortnight of the end of treatment. Thereafter, contact was maintained with those patients and their 'collateral informants', or 'significant others'. Post-treatment follow-ups were conducted at six weeks, six months, one and two years. At these times information was collected on the patient's drinking and occupational status, his use of therapeutic support outside the hospital, together with information by the collateral informant on the patient's current general interpersonal adjustment and ability to cope with stressful circumstances, compared with the year before hospitalization. Three descriptors were available: 'improved', 'same', or 'worse'.

Before turning to the results, it is important to be aware of the way in which drinking status, or 'disposition' was characterized, since this is the measure of therapeutic outcome that is likely to be of most immediate interest. 'Drunk days' were defined as those days on which at least 10 ounces, or their equivalent, of 86°-proof alcohol were consumed, or three or more consecutive days on which the daily consumption was between 7 to 9 ounces. 'Controlled drinking days' were those days on which no more than 6 ounces were consumed, or any isolated one- or two-day sequence when 7 to 9 were drunk. 'Abstinent days' were those on which no alcohol was consumed, enforced abstinent days (resulting from hospitalization or incarceration) being separately categorized.

The programme achieved the desired effects while the patients were hospitalized. The non-drinking experimental group ordered fewer drinks as treatment proceeded until, by session ten, no drinks were being ordered or consumed. Interestingly, some subjects did drink during the 'probe' (no shock) sessions, although throughout, prompting non-drinking patients to drink did not result in increased drinking. The controlled-drinking experimental group consistently drank as required, with very few inappropriate infringements of the rules. Seven of the 20 patients never received a single shock, while another seven received only one or two. The greatest number of shocks received (infringements perpetrated) by an individual patient was six. As with the abstinent group, probe sessions occasioned an increase in drinking but the average for the group was still less than 3 ounces per patient. Encouraging as these results are, the important question is whether the gains were maintained after the patients were discharged from hospital. The results at one- and two-year follow-ups will now be considered.

Throughout the follow-up period, each subject was contacted at three- to four-week intervals, as were as many collateral sources of information as possible.

Follow-up data collected with this frequency should obviously be less subject to memory-induced distortions than less frequently collected data. Public records, including court proceedings, incarcerations, traffic violations and hospitalization were checked for each patient every 2 months. Overall, the breadth of the follow-up data, the frequency of data collection are most impressive. Again, it is amazing that, given the geographical mobility of some patients, only one (from the controlled-drinking control group) could not be located at 19- to 24-month follow-up. Anyone who has attempted to collect follow-up data will appreciate what a feat it was for the Sobells to be able to report such comprehensive and complete data.

During the first year, the mean percentage of the time spent by the controlled-drinking groups in various drinking dispositions are shown in Table 7. The results show that although both groups spent the same amount of time incarcerated, they were markedly different in the other respects, with the experimental group spending more time drinking with control, more time abstinent and less time drunk than the control group. The Individualized Behaviour Therapy (IBT) clearly had a major impact on the ('experimental') patients who received it.

The corresponding results for the non-drinking groups are shown in Table 8.

Both groups spent about the same amount of their time

Table 7

Drinking disposition	Controlled drinking groups	
	Experimental	Control
Controlled drinking	25	10
Abstinent, but not incarcerated	45	26
Drunk	14	50
Incarcerated in hospital or gaol	16	15

NB. The figures have been rounded off.

Table 8

| | Non-drinking groups | |
Drinking disposition	Experimental	Control
Controlled drinking	3	6
Abstinent, but not incarcerated	65	32
Drunk	14	40
Incarcerated in hospital or gaol	17	22

NB. The figures have been rounded off.

incarcerated, but, in all other respects they differed. Of particular note is the fact that the experimental group spent twice as much time as the control group abstinent, and only one third as much of the time drunk. The experimental group showed the benefits of having undergone the IBT programme.

When the results from all four groups were compared, the similarity between the two control groups is evident, both having received only the standard hospital treatment. The experimental groups spent almost identical proportions of their time drunk, and incarcerated, but displayed two striking differences. The controlled-drinking experimental group spent much more of their time engaged in controlled drinking, whereas the non-drinking experimental group spent much more time abstinent. This is entirely consistent with the differences in treatment that the two groups received. If controlled-drinking and non-incarcerated abstinences are regarded as appropriate drinking dispositions, the controlled-drinking experimental group spent 70 per cent of its time behaving adaptively, and the non-drinking experimental group 68 per cent of its time.

Given that drinking behaviour is but one (important) measure of therapeutic outcome, it is interesting to note that in general adjustment, as perceived by the patients' collaterals, more of the two experimental groups showed improvements than in the control groups, with the controlled-drinking experimental group being better in this respect than the corresponding non-drinking group. More of both experimental groups showed vocational improvements than their corresponding controls, while more of the two experimental groups were in full or part-time employment than were their controls. Overall, the experimental groups fared much better over the first follow-up year in all respects, than did their corresponding control groups. As expected, the drinking dispositions of the experimental groups reflected the therapeutic goals towards which they had worked. Finally, the controlled-drinking experimental group were most improved in their general adjustment, as reported by their collateral information sources.

The results from the second-year follow-up showed that the patients in the controlled-drinking experimental group functioned significantly better in all respects than did the control group counterparts. The results are shown in Table 9, below. The experimental group was clearly functioning better than the control group. Comparing these two-year results with their one-year equivalents, some interesting changes are evident. The experimental group spent a similar proportion of its time drinking with control, but, during the second year, these patients spent a greater proportion of their time abstinent. There was no change in the proportion of time spent drunk, but the amount of time spent incarcerated fell dramatically in the

Table 9

	Controlled drinking groups	
Drinking disposition	Experimental	Control
Controlled drinking	23	6
Abstinent, but not incarcerated	63	36
Drunk	12	49
Incarcerated in hospital or gaol	3	8

NB. The figures have been rounded off.

second year. The control group results show that less time was spent drinking with control, but more time was spent abstinent. The high proportion of drunken days remained unchanged, while time incarcerated fell by almost half. Overall, both groups showed some improvement in drinking disposition, although this was more pronounced for the experimental group.

The second-year non-drinking group results are shown in Table 10. The experimental group appears to have been functioning better than its control counterpart, both groups spending a greater proportion of the time abstinent than either drunk or drinking with control. Comparing the first- and second-year results for these groups, the main differences are that the experimental group spent a greater proportion of its time drunk in the second year, whereas the control group spent more time abstinent. When the second-year results for all four groups are compared, it is evident that the group with the best and most adaptive drinking disposition was the controlled-drinking experimental group.

Table 10

Drinking dispositions	Non-drinking groups	
	Experimental	Control
Controlled drinking	4	2
Abstinent, but not incarcerated	61	42
Drunk	20	37
Incarcerated in hospital or gaol	15	19

NB. The figures have been rounded off.

Turning to the second-year collateral data, the controlled-drinking experimental group was functioning better, on all measures, than any of the other three groups. Furthermore, this group improved on these measures in the second year. The collateral data for the non-drinking group showed a deterioration in general adjustment, vocational and occupational status, and less use of therapeutic supports. However, although the differences between the two controlled-drinking groups were statistically different during each six-month period over the two-year follow-up period, the differences between the two non-drinking groups were not statistically significant during the second year. Simply stated, the experimental controlled-drinking group was consistently 'better adjusted' than its control group, whereas the effects of treatment on the non-drinking experimental group ceased to be significant in the second year.

A number of criticisms have been levelled against the Sobells' study, so I shall mention a few here. Although there is no doubt that the subjects were suffering from the alcohol dependence syndrome (they were 'alcoholics' in the sense that they conformed to the Jellinek's (1960) definition of 'Gamma' alcoholics), they were not randomly assigned to the treatment groups. (Random assignment is a requirement of classic experimental designs.) The patients had some influence over the treatment goals assigned to them. Likewise, the controlled-drinking groups had to have social support that would encourage controlled drinking, whereas any patient who lacked such support was automatically assigned to the non-drinking groups. The important conclusion that must be drawn from this is that the controlled-drinking patients started with better prognoses than their non-drinking group peers. The clear implication is that the result of the study can safely be generalized only to alcoholics who conform to the selection criteria used in this study. It cannot be assumed that all alcoholics would benefit equally from engaging in the controlled-drinking programme, and the Sobells have been careful to make this very point (1973a). The follow-up procedure was intensive, hence the completeness of the reported data. However, as the Sobells (1973b) made clear, the question arises whether this frequency of follow-up contact itself functioned as a form of after-care for some patients. The outcome criteria have provided a major source of debate. Throughout the two years of follow-up, all four groups spent a proportion of their days 'drunk'. The lowest mean percentage (12) of 'drunk' days was achieved by the controlled-drinking experimental group during the second year of follow-up. It could be objected that since, by definition, this is not controlled drinking, the treatment package had failed. This was the stance taken by Ewing and Rouse (1976) when they reported their 'failure' to inculcate controlled drinking in their patients. During the 27 to 55 month follow-ups, it was found that all the patients had experienced uncontrolled-drinking episodes. On these grounds, Ewing and Rouse described the therapeutic outcome as a 'failure', because their criterion for success was an absolute and indefinitely continuing absence of uncontrolled drinking. They explicitly stated that a single 'loss of control' incident would constitute a therapeutically poor outcome. True, other considerations were also mentioned by these authors but, in my view, their criterion for success is too narrow. Perfection is unattainable. Abstinence-oriented treatments typically produce outcomes that include bouts of uncontrolled drinking, but are not then construed as failures. It is generally accepted that social drinking patterns sometimes include brief uncontrolled episodes. True, the implications of such an episode may be different for social drinkers and alcoholics, but the fact remains that social drinking is characterized in a way that admits some 'deviant' behaviour. If, as the Sobells have shown with their sample, the best overall outcome was achieved by the controlled-drinking experimental group, these results cannot be dismissed.

High-quality research is needed to determine, first, the best bases on which to assign therapeutic goals to individual patients and, second, the most potentially beneficial therapeutic programme for each patient. Evaluation of such research would have to sample many aspects of the individual's functioning (it would have to be multidimensional) and, ideally, there would be general agreement over outcome criteria.

On the assumption that the reader has not cast this book aside in response to the welter of detail provided above, the complexity of the issues surrounding the matter of controlled-drinking treatment should now be abundantly clear. Any blanket statements that controlled drinking or abstinence-oriented goals are the 'best' for 'alcoholics' can be dismissed out of hand. If the reader now understands why that is so, this overlong account will have achieved its aim.

Maintenance of therapeutic gains

In the early days there was a tendency for treatment agencies to consider their work complete once the alcoholic had undergone treatment. The tacit assumption seems to have been that, given a fresh start, it was then solely up to the patient to make the most of it. It is now recognized that, in most instances, this is an unrealistic viewpoint. Maintaining and improving on the gains made during treatment is now recognized as a necessary part of the total therapeutic effort. Follow-up or 'booster' sessions are often arranged to enhance maintenance. It will be recalled that Voegtlin and Broz (1949) and Lemere and Voegtlin (1950) scheduled booster sessions 6 and 12 months after the completion of their chemical aversion therapy, but additional boosters were available to patients, on request. It was mentioned, above, in connection with the Sobells' study that the frequent follow-ups may have acted as maintenance sessions for some of the patients. A widely used procedure is to arrange maintenance sessions at increasingly long intervals following treatment, so that the frequency of therapeutic contacts is gradually reduced as time passes. This allows the therapist gradually to withdraw support in proportion to the extent that the patient is able to assume full command. This all amounts to a transitional phase of treatment. It should be borne in mind that this period of readjustment, or 'rehabilitation', usually throws up new problems, some of which will fall outside any one therapist's area of competence. This is but one reason why a multidisciplinary team approach to the treatment and aftercare of alcoholics is desirable. The reader will remember that Hunt and Azrin's (1973) Community Reinforcement treatment package included setting up a social club for patients and ex-patients as part of their maintenance programme. Again, their treatment involved attempts to improve the alcoholic's family, financial, occupational and leisure time functioning to aid maintenance. Many alcoholics fail to maintain and build upon their therapeutic gains, unless strenuous efforts are made to assist them in that task. It is for this reason that a variety of aftercare methods and agencies have emerged.

Pride of place for aftercare should probably go to Alcoholics Anonymous. Maintenance, through regular attendance at meetings, the 24-hour availability of a telephone counselling service, and support through visits from other members if the alcoholic feels a strong urge to drink, can be regarded as maintenance components. Add to this the fact that AA branches are scattered throughout Britain, North America and Canada, and one begins to appreciate why, in terms of coverage and availability, AA maintenance should take pride of place. A plausible objection might be that there is no circumscribed AA treatment package, so post-therapy maintenance is a meaningless concept. Even so, many AA members readily admit that regular attendance at meetings, and 'twelve-stepping' (visiting and providing support at the request of alcoholics who believe themselves to be in danger of drinking, or who have already done so), helps them to maintain their sobriety.

A more formal means of providing a transitional phase between treatment and full, independent social functioning is available in the form of what are broadly referred to as 'halfway houses'. It is a measure of the number of such houses that FARE (the Federation of Alcoholism Rehabilitation Establishments) was established. A halfway house provides residential accommodation and, often, a counselling or therapeutic programme, for alcoholics who have undergone formal treatment in a hospital or alcoholism unit. Those with a strong therapeutic component may accommodate alcoholics who have not undergone hospital treatment, but these are then therapeutic agencies in their own right. The important feature of halfway houses is that they are intended to provide the opportunity for a smoother transition from hospital or unit back into the community. Thus, the houses are community based, permitting the residents to try out and develop the coping skills they learned while in formal treatment. Housekeeping, shopping, cooking, in fact the whole business of running the household is often the responsibility of the residents, although some houses have resident 'leaders' or 'managers', and some may well boast their own housekeepers and cooks. The ultimate target is to enable the resident to return to fully independent living in the community.

Another type of maintenance or rehabilitation development is referred to as a 'day-centre'. These are community-based establishments in which alcoholics can spend time during the day and, sometimes, the evening. Some Alcoholism Information Centres provide a room, or rooms, for this purpose. Day centres usually provide a 'walk-in' service, so that an alcoholic is free to drop in for shorter or longer periods. Some provide counselling services and some act as referral agencies through which access to the therapeutic services can be achieved. In addition to these features, a day centre may provide television, radio, games of various sorts, handicraft work, and so forth.

In summary, a variety of maintenance, or rehabilitation, facilities exist which can provide varying degrees of support for alcoholics who have completed treatment. Some are hybrids, in that they may also be treatment agencies in their own right, whereas others provide more general support for as long as the individual avails him or herself of their services.

Having at last come to the end of this long chapter, certain general conclusions can be discerned. As Emrick (1975) pointed out, it is better for an alcoholic to be treated than not to be treated. He also concluded that it does not seem to matter which treatment one chooses, since there is little evidence that one is better than another. From the patient's point of view, this is good news, although the therapist may feel a little piqued. Since Emrick was taking an overview of several hundred different studies, no doubt his general conclusions are valid. Recent work by Hunt and Azrin (1973) and the Sobells (1973a,b; 1976) does suggest that some methods have better 'success' rates than is more generally the case. The familiar complaint that 'more and better research is needed' is nowhere truer than in the case of alcoholism treatments. There is also a growing conviction that we should be paying more attention to prevention, so it is to that topic that I now turn in the next and final chapter.

Chapter 11

Future developments

In this final chapter I shall consider four topics, including prevention, detection, treatment and research.

Prevention

Although at least three types of prevention have been described, I am here concerned solely with the 'primary' or absolute prevention of alcohol-related problems. The question is how may alcohol-related problems be prevented from ever occurring? The simple answer is that absolute prevention is quite impossible. This is probably one of the few things over which there is likely to be agreement between those engaged in preventive endeavours. A more realistic goal is to identify ways of reducing the incidence of alcohol-related problems. Various means have been proposed, from the draconian to the mild, but, one way or another, society has to decide what is an acceptable incidence of these problems. Currently, the scale of the problem has not fully entered public awareness, so that the majority of the population is unaffected and unaware. Raising public consciousness on the subject of drinking is one preventive step that can and, to some extent, is being taken, but any single approach to prevention is unlikely to succeed on its own. I shall consider a variety of preventive measures although, to have a significant impact, any worthwhile programme would have to be multidimensional, continual and, probably, of national scope.

Prohibition

The simplest and most obvious preventive measure would be totally to prohibit the sale and consumption of alcohol. Moslem countries, such as Saudi Arabia, have prohibition laws, and severe punishments can be meted out to those caught infringing the laws. Although infringements do occur, it seems that prohibition is widely observed in these countries because alcohol is proscribed by the state religion. Legal, secular prohibition supports the religious requirement of abstinence from alcohol. In contrast, attempts to impose prohibition fail in countries where drinking is common and where there is no widely observed state religion that demands abstinence. The American experience provides a paradigm example. In 1920, the 18th Amendment to the Constitution imposed 'Prohibition' on the nation. In 1933, that Amendment was repealed because it had proved to be unworkable. It never achieved popular support and it spawned a wave of organized crime that rocked the country. Interestingly, although there is still an active temperance movement in Britain, it seeks support from individuals rather than lobbying for legal prohibition. In summary, unless there is widespread popular support for prohibition, any attempt to impose it must fail. Widespread support for prohibition does not exist in Western countries and is not, therefore, a practical method of prevention.

Fiscal measures

It is well established that as the true cost of alcohol falls, per capita consumption rises. This is most often expressed in terms of the price of alcohol as a percentage of the mean weekly per capita disposable income. In round terms, when alcohol is relatively cheap, there is a clear trend towards heavier drinking. The obvious conclusion is that one way of reducing the average consumption level is by increasing the real price of the beverage. Demand is usually reduced when the true cost of a product rises significantly (Popham *et al.* 1975). Equally, by maintaining the real cost of alcohol at a constant level, the mean individual level of consumption would be expected to remain constant. The latter, milder, measure was advocated by the Advisory Committee on Alcoholism (of the DHSS and Welsh Office) in a report on prevention (Advisory Committee on Alcoholism 1978). Politically, this is likely to be more acceptable to the electorate than the tougher measure of increasing the real cost and maintaining it at a high level. As Popham *et al.* remarked, the more radical option would probably have to be preceded by a public education programme to make the measure effective and politically possible. Notice that references to the cost of 'alcohol' means 'alcohol' but not 'beverage'. The real taxation on beverages would be in direct proportion to their alcohol content. In Britain, the revenue on spirits is much higher than on the equivalent volume of beer.

Several doubts and objections have been raised over this matter concerning, for example, the undiscriminating nature of taxation. Consider the example of two drinkers with similar consumption levels but widely different disposable incomes. The lower-paid drinker would be relatively harder hit by any increase in the real cost of alcohol than would the higher-paid individual. There is no practical way of avoiding this state of affairs, since it applies to all commodities. The important issue is whether society would accept fiscal measures of this sort, in the expectation of reducing alcohol consumption and, hence, the incidence of alcohol-related problems. It has been objected that home brewing would increase if commercially-produced beverages were made unacceptably expensive. I know of no empirical evidence that supports this view, but it seems unlikely to occur to any great extent if the increases in taxation were gradually introduced. It might be objected that severe fiscal measures would cause massive problems for those who already exhibit the Alcohol Dependence Syndrome. A counter argument is that this might motivate them to seek treatment. As discussed earlier in this book, there is strong evidence that alcoholics can and do adjust their consumption, depending on their financial status at the time. To argue that society should make it *easy* for the alcohol dependent to remain dependent, seems unreasonable.

It may have occurred to the reader that raising the real cost of alcohol could be accomplished without increasing the cost *of the beverage* to the consumer. This could be achieved by reducing the amount of alcohol in the beverage, so that the cost of the remaining alcohol would have been raised. True, some drinkers would compensate by drinking more of their chosen beverage, thus maintaining their consumption of alcohol. The main preventive impact would be on those who habitually drink a fixed quantity of beverage. The two-pint-a-day drinker could maintain that liquid intake but would automatically be consuming less alcohol. A reduction in the alcohol (proof) content of vodka has been tried in Russia (Grant 1979).

Licensing: establishments and hours

One possible means of reducing the mean per capita alcohol consumption would be by severely reducing the number of licensed retail premises. Essentially the idea is one of making alcohol more difficult to obtain in the expectation that people will drink less. No doubt ease of availability is one factor that influences drinking practices but there is no evidence that it is a major variable. (Total prohibition provides an extreme case that will not be considered here.) Laying in a stock of drink would be the most obvious answer to any restriction that might be made on availability. The second possibility would be to restrict licensing hours; that is, the hours during which alcohol can be sold in a retail establishment. If taken too far, the result could be other than one might wish. Those who drink in licensed premises might simply drink the same quantity of alcohol faster, a practice that is known to have various undesirable consequences. A dramatic example of what can be achieved by licensing occurred in Britain in the First World War. Drunkenness amongst munitions workers resulted in a scarcity of arms for the fighting services. The effects of imposing restrictive licensing hours included very pronounced reductions in the consumption of beer and spirits, in alcoholic mortality and drunkenness rates. Although conscription into the armed services took many young male drinkers out of circulation, the evidence strongly suggests that the new licensing hours were the major determinant of the above reductions. Reducing the number of retail outlets that are licensed to sell alcohol, and imposing more restrictive licensing hours are unlikely to occur, in view of the current trend towards greater liberalization of drinking controls (Smith 1981b). Presumably, in response to this trend, the Special Committee of the Royal College of Psychiatrists (1979) included a specific recommendation in their report urging that the current licensing provisions should undergo no further relaxation. Likewise, the earlier report of the Advisory Committee on Alcoholism (1978) made specific recommendations that licensing restrictions should be 'rigorously' enforced and that they should not be relaxed until there is good evidence that no harm would result.

Advertising

It was reported in Chapter 3 that in 1979 six major brewers spent nearly £17.5 million on advertising their products. This was but part of the total sum spent on such advertising by all the interested parties. Even so, that figure is nearly 1,000 times as much as the Health Education Council spent on campaigns publicizing the effects of alcohol abuse. The contest, if it can be thus characterized, is undeniably one-sided. Alcohol advertisements are carefully orchestrated to project predetermined images of particular drinks and those who drink them. This is true of all good advertising, whatever the product. All the skills of the advertising industry are used to induce potential, to become actual, customers, and to enhance brand loyalty. Naturally, the message is always positive. Does the reader recall any instance in which an advertisement for a particular alcoholic beverage included a caution about the potentially harmful consequences of over indulgence? I very much doubt it. There already exists the precedent in Britain. Cigarette packets must carry a 'government health warning' to the effect that smoking can damage one's health. Restrictions have also been placed on cigarette advertising on television. These measures have been implemented, at least in part, in response to the pressure exerted on government over the last two decades by the strong anti-smoking lobby. There is evidence that cigarette smoking has declined, although the causes for this go beyond any one factor. Would similar restrictions on alcohol advertisements be rewarded by similar reductions in consumption? Unfortunately, the evidence relating to this question is equivocal. Ogborne and Smart (1980) considered the results of restricting alcohol advertising in Manitoba and British Columbia, and examined the relationships between the extent of such advertising restrictions and per capita alcohol consumption, and alcoholism rates in 51 American States. They concluded that advertising restrictions are unlikely to result in reduced alcohol consumption. In an econometric study of United Kingdom data, Duffy (1981) found a weak association between advertising and the demand for beer and spirits, but none for wine demand. Overall, advertising seems to have little if any influence on alcohol demand, and no studies have been published in which a strong influence has been detected. The UK Code of Advertising Standards does have a section on alcohol which explicitly attempts to prevent young people from becoming specific marketing targets.

It additionally precludes advertising in which social and sexual success are associated with drinking. Infringements of the Code carry no penalties, because adherence to it on the part of advertisers is entirely voluntary. Smith (1981b) struck a timely note of warning against dismissing as irrelevant restrictions on alcohol advertising. He drew attention to the difficulty of measuring the effects of advertising restrictions, while additionally pointing out that health education advertising is negated by the much more extensive and continual alcohol advertising. Despite the paucity of evidence that advertising affects the sale of alcohol, Smith noted that, on tactical grounds, the anti-alcohol abuse lobby might do well to campaign against advertising. A campaign of that type would be unlikely to arouse public antipathy, it would have a symbolic value, and it could provide a vehicle for other anti-abuse messages. The Advisory Committee on Alcoholism (1978) recommended that steps should be taken to ensure that the public is presented with a more balanced account of the effects of alcohol. The Special Committee of the Royal College of Psychiatrists (1979) recommended that the government should initiate research into the consequences of alcohol advertising and if the evidence demanded it it should curtail such advertising.

Education

The best means of prevention in a rational society is through education. If it is to be successful, health education must be continual, it must provide convincing information that can be understood by most of the population, and it must be adequately funded. The task of organising, orchestrating and maintaining an educational programme of a worthwhile sort would be considerable. Bear in mind that the programme would need to comprise a package of programmes targeted on the entire population as well as on sub-groups. Different programmes would be needed for children in primary and secondary education while, at the other extreme, adults in occupations that carry a high risk of drinking problems would require quite different packages. Although a major part of the total programme would be concerned with those who already drink, no doubt different age groups, different ethnic groups, and even the two sexes would best be served by programmes designed specifically for them. Commerce, industry and the trades unions could, and should, be involved in this type of preventive health education. Long-running radio and television serials could provide suitable vehicles for a general programme of alcohol education (Advisory Committee on Alcoholism 1978). The British radio serial, the 'Archers', provides information to farmers on new legislation, new methods, and so forth while, at the same time, providing entertainment. All this sounds expensive, and if it was intended to carry it out on a scale that was large enough to ensure a good chance of success, it probably would be 'expensive'. The cost to the country of alcohol abuse has already been mentioned in this book, but what guarantee would we have that money spent on prevention would result in a net saving?

It must be admitted that no valid guarantees could be given. Proposals for preventive programmes always face the problem of demonstrating that they can be cost-effective in the long run. A few studies have recently been published in which the effectiveness of small-scale, primary prevention programmes has been evaluated. Kim (1981) reported a successful outcome with over 1,000 school children from a primary prevention programme on drug abuse. The drug abuse of those who had participated in the 'Ombudsman' programme was compared with those who had not been involved. The greatest impact was on the young children (however, fewer of all age groups who had undergone the programme were found to be using 'hard' drugs than those children who had not, but a significantly smaller proportion of the Ombudsman participants were found not to be using hard drugs than of those who had not undergone the programme). Interestingly, there were no significant differences between the two groups in their use of 'social' drugs such as tobacco, alcohol and marijuana. Although, as the author admits, the research methodology was less than perfect, this was useful and encouraging pioneering work.

Ultimately, any nationally implemented primary prevention programme of the sort alluded to above would almost certainly be an expensive act of faith. It could hardly be otherwise in a society in which alcohol has, traditionally, been widely used and highly valued. Any educational programme would have to contend with deep-rooted traditional beliefs and practices concerning alcohol. Drinking alcohol is more than a means of quenching one's thirst. That very fact marks the beginning of the difficulties facing all who support the preventive enterprise in this field.

Detection

However good preventive measures may be, it is certain that some drinkers will fall foul of drinking problems. Some will recognize that their drinking is becoming problematic and will take appropriate steps to remedy that. Some will not recognize the alcohol-relatedness of their problems, while others will recognize it but do nothing about it. Public health education should eventually raise awareness to the point where more sufferers will recognize the immediate source of their problems, and more will also seek help. It is a basic rule that early treatment of any problem carried a better prognosis than treatment that is delayed. Early detection and treatment of an individual's drinking problem is, therefore, of the utmost importance. Putting it at its mildest, there is much room for improvement in the matter of early detection. Society is reluctant to identify excessive drinking as exactly that. The person who drinks 8 pints of beer, or half a bottle of whisky every day 'Likes a *good* drink'. The employee who always has a hangover on Monday mornings 'Is a bit of a lad for the booze'. Drinking usually has to be habitually very visibly excessive before others label it as such. Even then, most people would be reluctant to broach the subject with the drinker. Suitable education, leading to changes in the public's perception of drinking problems, would be one step towards early detection and confrontation. This implies a considerable change in public attitudes. The Special Committee of the Royal College of Psychiatrists (1979) makes the recommendation that nobody should ignore the fact that an individual is drinking excessively, but should respond as they would in the case of any other potentially dangerous behaviour.

Trades unions and employers in North America have long been involved in occupational alcoholism programmes. These have sometimes been run solely by a union, sometimes only by the employer. In a review of the responses to alcoholism by unions, Johnson, (1981) commented that joint programmes are usually to be preferred, although this is sometimes difficult to achieve. The Health and Safety Executive booklet 'The problem drinker at work' (1981) provides a set of guidelines for, and advocates that, employers should establish and operate a policy to assist problem drinking employees. Although joint involvement of unions and employers is recommended, the guidelines suggest that the effective operation of the policy should be the responsibility of at least one member of the senior management. More important, it is stressed that the policy should apply to all members of the organization, regardless of their position within the company hierarchy. An important goal of the suggested policy is to make it easy for those with drinking problems to seek help. Drinking problems are to be regarded in the same way as any other 'illness'. The general (and laudable) purpose of the guidelines is to encourage all concerned to approach drinking problems in a rational and compassionate and positive manner. It remains to be seen whether the guidelines will be implemented on anything like the scale necessary to make a significant contribution towards reducing the high cost of employees' problem drinking.

Professional training is the last topic that I shall mention in connection with detection. The available estimates all suggest that many problem drinkers go undetected. This is understandable when the problem is at an early stage of development, but it seems that even well-established problems are overlooked by those professionals who should be able to recognize the tell-tale signs. Lack of knowledge is an obvious cause and that is surely a sufficient explanation in some cases. The most effective long-term solution would be to ensure that the training programmes for certain 'caring' professions include the theory and practice of identifying clients or patients who have drinking problems. The list of professions would certainly include medicine, psychiatry, health visiting, nursing of all types, clinical psychology, social and probation work, to name only a few. Several screening questionnaires have been developed to assist in detecting alcoholics. Wilkins (1974), a general practitioner, has developed a questionnaire that can be used to identify general practice patients who are likely to be experiencing drinking problems. Why is it that, to the best of my knowledge, this potentially useful diagnostic procedure has not been widely used by general practitioners or any other health care professionals? Although not attempting to answer this question, Lisansky (1974) has speculated about why alcoholism is an 'avoided diagnosis'. For example, the typical middle-class, professional ethics of delayed gratification, self-control, and social responsibility, are polar opposites of the picture presented by many alcoholic patients. Lisansky believes that as a consequence of these differences between therapist and patient, physicians have difficulty in empathizing with alcoholics and, in practice, prefer to avoid treating them. A further reason why physicians may 'avoid' diagnosing alcoholism, is that alcoholics have a reputation for being unco-operative patients. Doubtless there are many interacting reasons why 'alcoholism' may be an avoided diagnosis. Education, at the public health and professional training levels, should go a long way towards correcting this situation.

Treatment

Although prevention is better than cure, there will always be those with drinking problems who will need treatment. Certain fundamental questions must be resolved by all therapists when confronted by a patient who is seeking help. First, the 'problem' must be identified and under-stood in its several aspects. We have seen that alcoholism influences many, if not all, aspects of the individual's life; similarly, its maintenance is the result of many interacting factors. It is apparent that 'understanding' the problem calls for a well-developed range of clinical skills. The reader will recall, however, that empirical evidence has already been presented showing that even treatment of a minimal kind is better than no treatment at all. In view of this finding, is there really a need for the comprehensive understanding, referred to above? The answer, as with so many things, is that: 'It depends!' It depends on several factors, two of the most important being the therapeutic goal and the available treatments. (Of course, these two factors interact.) If, for whatever reasons, the most appropriate goal in a particular case is a minimal one, it is likely that this could be decided without a comprehensive understanding of the patient's problem, and by means of minimal treatment. A paradigm example would be that of many elderly Skid Row alcoholics. Assuming that such a patient was not motivated to do anything about the excessive drinking, there would be little point in trying to understand that problem in all its tortuous complexity, The most appropriate 'treatment' might then be no more than advice to maintain some food intake every day, and to drink alcoholic beverages rather than methylated spirits. Another patient might request the goal of controlled drinking which, before it could be agreed by the therapist, would require a thorough understanding of that patient's background and lifestyle in its broadest sense. If it was mutually agreed to pursue that goal, a relatively complex multidimensional treatment package would probably be required. The components of the package would be chosen in the light of a comprehensive understanding of the patient's problem. In such a case, minimal treatment would almost certainly be inappropriate. The reader will probably be aware of at least three unstated problems in the latter example. First, the definition of 'controlled drinking' has not been included, no mention was made of the criteria used for selecting the treatment goals, and none for the treatment components.

Currently, there is no generally agreed definition of 'controlled drinking'. It would be helpful if an index of controlled drinking could be developed, so that the outcomes from different treatment studies should be directly compared. As I have tried to indicate, above, even the seemingly straightforward goal of 'abstinence' presents difficulties, since absolute abstinence does not entail adequate adjustment in other areas of personal functioning. 'Abstinence' and 'controlled drinking' (however defined) refer only to drinking behaviour. They are necessary goals in the treatment of drinking problems but they are not sufficient on their own. Multidimensional goals are required if treatments are to be evaluated adequately. It follows that means must be developed for assessing the outcome of treatments in terms of those multifaceted goals.

The second unstated problem, that of the criteria to be used for selecting treatment goals, is difficult unless only a single goal is available. The problem is often easily resolved in extreme cases. The elderly, lifelong Skid Row alcoholic is generally agreed to have a very poor prognosis, and a majority of therapists would see no point in trying to involve this type of patient in an alcoholism treatment programme. On the other hand, 'shop fronts' represent one route by which some vagrant alcoholics can gain access to the treatment services. In many cases, overnight ('shelter'), longer term hotel accommodation or prison, are the only nearest thing to therapy experienced by this group. At the other extreme, the younger drinker has a good prognosis if he or she has a short history of excessive drinking, enjoys good family and social support that is not dependent on excessive drinking, is satisfactorily employed, has an earlier history of normal social drinking, and wishes to regain control over his or her excessive drinking. This latter type of patient would probably be accepted into treatment by a majority of therapists. As is so often the case, the majority of patients lie between these two extremes, so that deciding on the 'best' treatment goal is more difficult. Although the research literature provides some criteria by which appropriate goals can be chosen, they amount to 'rules of thumb'. Ultimately, however well a patient may or may not meet the criteria for a particular treatment goal, the therapist may reject that goal, even though available as a result of his or her 'clinical judgement'. This is an amalgam of many variables, including one's experience as a therapist, one's knowledge of the theoretical and empirical research literature, knowledge gained from discussions with colleagues, and one's own 'hunch' or best guess about the extent to which a particular patient would achieve a particular treatment goal. The criteria for selecting appropriate treatment goals need to be established through empirical research.

The third unstated question concerns the selection of treatment package components. Two separate but related issues are involved. The effectiveness of various treatments in achieving their intended goal needs to be established. If abstinence is the chosen goal for a particular patient, it is incumbent upon the therapist to use the most effective ethically acceptable means of helping the patient achieve that goal. Unfortunately, a treatment that is highly effective with one patient may be less effective, or ineffective, with another. This difference may result from the lifestyle of the two individuals, from differences between them in personality, intelligence, drinking history, age, available interpersonal or social or family support, and so on. Matching patients with treatments to achieve the best outcome is currently more a matter of art than of science. The problem is not unique to treating excessive drinking. A choice of drugs is usually available for treating any particular bodily disease. The choice of drug for an individual patient may be based on a number of considerations. Young babies are likely to swallow liquids more easily than solids. Liquids are then the form in which the drug is administered, if it is to be given by mouth. Some individuals are known to be allergic to certain drugs, such as penicillin. Physicians always enquire whether their patient is allergic to a particular class of drugs before prescribing them. If the patient does not know, he or she will be cautioned that if certain symptoms occur no more of that drug should be taken and the patient should return. In addition, drugs are sometimes more effective with some people than with others. The physician may have to try treating the illness with a sequence of drugs, until an effective one is found for a particular patient. This procedure usually takes a few days or weeks. In contrast, the treatment of alcoholism usually takes weeks and an initially good outcome may eventually deteriorate. Opinion is divided on the point at which the overall outcome can be evaluated with confidence, but between two and five years after treatment ends is probably about right. One can appreciate that it could take years to try out a sequence of alcoholism treatment packages on even one patient. Furthermore, repeated failures would take their toll of the patient. While not denying that programmes can be, and are, adjusted during the course of treatment, it is important to begin with a treatment strategy that is as nearly 'correct' as possible for the patient in question.

The fact that initially successful outcomes can sometimes deteriorate during the follow-up period has been mentioned. The problem of maintaining treatment gains, or 'maintenance', is common to clinical psychology, psychiatry and social work, to name but three disciplines. It may be that the treatment packages devised by Hunt and Azrin (1973) and the Sobells (1973) owed some of their long-term success to built-in maintenance procedures. This seems undeniably to be so in the case of the Community Reinforcement approach. The situation is less clear with regard to Individualized Behaviour Therapy but, as Sobell and Sobell (1973a) pointed out, the frequent data collection contacts may have served as a form of maintenance procedure. Other more formal maintenance strategies have also been used. In the 1940s, Voegtlin and co-workers scheduled 'booster' sessions for their chemical aversion treatment patients during the follow-up period. Regular telephone and postal contacts can also be used to monitor progress and to detect any deterioration at an early stage. The factor common to all these maintenance methods is extended therapeutic contact. The intensive treatment during the initial therapeutic package is followed by non-intensive intermittent therapeutic contacts. The exception is the Hunt and Azrin (1973) programme which involves continuous maintenance, although contacts with the therapist do decline in frequency. No matter how initially successful treatment is, effective maintenance procedures are essential. It is probably true that the majority of treatment research has been concerned with initial interventions. One disincentive to carrying out research on maintenance is that it involves a considerable commitment of time and effort, extending over several years. Special incentives may be necessary if this important work is to be carried out. Ultimately, it is most likely to be undertaken by organizations that are heavily committed to research, such as institutions of higher education and government-funded research units.

A comparatively recent approach to maintenance involves 'self-management'. Treatment has traditionally been 'delivered' to the patient. This is seen in its purest form, for example, in the case of vaccinations; the patient is called upon to do no more than present him or herself for vaccination. Minimal involvement is required of the patient. The treatment of alcoholism has always required the active participation of the patient but, still, treatment has largely been directed by the therapist. First, self-management procedures aim to provide the alcoholic with the skills to identify the factors that have led to the onset and maintenance of excessive drinking, and to recognize new factors that might lead to similar problems. Second, self-management includes teaching the individual how to modify his or her responses to those factors, or 'antecedents', so that more effective coping strategies than excessive drinking become available. Expressing it in a more dramatic way, the alcoholic is provided with the means to control his or her own behaviour. Hence, these procedures are sometimes referred to as 'self-control' strategies. A large part of the Sobells' Individualized Behaviour Therapy approach comprised self-management training. The theoretical and, when successful, practical advantage of teaching self-management skills is that maintenance is assured. Without wishing to become too enmeshed in a discussion of this topic, the maintenance of self-management procedures cannot be assumed, so this becomes an additional area in which research is required.

Although I shall do no more than mention them, here, half-way-houses also represent a means by which the maintenance of therapeutic gains is sought. Likewise, Alcoholics Anonymous certainly provides the longest term maintenance that is available, many members continuing their active participation over many years or several decades. Maintenance of this duration, on both a national and international scale, is most unlikely to be provided by anything other than a voluntary agency, so it is to this topic that I now turn.

Voluntary or non-statutory agencies such as Alcoholics Anonymous, the National Council on Alcoholism, and the hostel movement provide a major input to the treatment and aftercare of alcoholics. It is clear that many people with drinking problems do gain much from their involvement with these organizations. Thus, some patients do well without treatment from professionally qualified therapists. Professionals might have something to offer their voluntary, non-statutory counterparts in the area of treatment monitoring and outcome evaluation. Likewise, some of the professional therapist's clinical skills could be made available and, most important, properly taught to non-professionals. A precedent already exists. 'Para-professional' 'nurse (behaviour) therapists' have been trained in the Institute of Psychiatry, in London, to treat some of the more commonly occurring psychological problems. Interestingly, their success rates equal and sometimes exceed those of professionally qualified therapists.

Co-operation between the voluntary and statutory treatment agencies already exists. This could be improved and extended in many ways, to the ultimate benefit of those seeking treatment for drinking problems.

Research

It is almost a convention that scientific reports, of all sorts, somewhere contain the invocation that 'more research is required'. Anyone with even a cursory knowledge of the alcoholism research literature would probably agree that, indeed, more research is certainly required in the areas of prevention, detection, treatment goal choice, treatment, maintenance and multidisciplinary approaches as well as female and adolescent drinking problems, to mention those that immediately spring to mind. This list could be greatly extended. The plain fact is that research on this scale requires a considerable human and financial investment. A rational approach would be to undertake joint research, in which several researchers or teams would co-operate on a single piece of research. This kind of enterprise is difficult to organize, partly due to logistical reasons, partly because it can take a long time to set up and partly, it must be admitted, because of 'personal' reasons. By 'personal' reasons I have in mind the autonomy that is cherished by so many researchers, the wish to receive full, unshared credit for a good piece of research, and the fact that multiple authorship research publications may carry less weight than single authorship reports. I am describing a mixture of personal predilection and factors that may influence career prospects. One way in which joint research might be encouraged would be for research funding bodies specifically to assign a proportion of their money to joint projects only.

Whether or not joint research becomes more usual in the field of alcoholism, there is a body of opinion in favour of a national planning agency. In theory nationally planned and co-ordinated research should cover more topics and provide more and faster answers than unco-ordinated, independently planned investigations. A national planning and co-ordinating agency for alcohol problems research could be envisaged, which would publish a list of research project that it was willing to fund. The results of such research would be fed back to the agency which, in the light of the emerging overall picture, would initiate further research projects. The general picture would be one of a rational, objective, wise and benign organization, whose sole purpose was to promote research that would answer the many questions that exist in the complex field of drinking problems. My guess is that it will be a very long time before an agency of this sort is established; if it ever happens. Readers will understand the fears that this type of agency could become a bureaucratic monstrosity, well short of the ideals outlined, above. 'Big' may not prove to be 'beautiful', or even desirable. Without going into details, several middle courses are feasible. There already exist government funded Research Councils which, apart from funding suitable research submitted to them by individual researchers and research teams, have their own autonomous research units. There is no reason why this sort of parallel funding should not be applied to drinking problems. In fact, the Research Councils have been and are involved in funding individual alcoholism research projects. If government funding were made available, alcoholism research units could be established to carry out long-term and other comparatively unpopular types of research. They could also act as co-ordinating centres for independently carried out investigations. It seems doubtful to me whether any of this will happen, unless initiated at national governmental level.

Ultimately, as with so many things, the level of funding largely determines the amount and quality of effort expended on research. British government advisers and organizations appear to be awakening to the size, complexity, cost and impact of drinking problems on all aspects of national life. There is no reason to believe that the scale of these problems will diminish, and many reasons to believe that they will increase, unless decisive action is initiated.

For my own part, I should be well pleased if some readers of this book are now more aware that a drinking problem of horrendous national proportions exists amongst us.

References

Adelstein, A. and White, G. (1976) *Population Trends Nos. 6 & 7*, London: HMSO.

Advisory Committee on Alcoholism (1978) *Report on prevention*. London: HMSO.

Ashen, B. and Donner, L. (1968) Covert sensitization with alcoholics: a controlled replication, *Behaviour Research and Therapy*, **6**, 7–12.

Benjamin, I. S., Imrie, C. W. and Blumgart, L. H. (1977) Alcohol and the pancreas. In G. Edwards and M. Grant (eds), *Alcoholism: new knowledge and new perspectives*. London: Croom Helm.

Berg, N. L. (1971) Effects of alcohol intoxication on self-concept: studies of alcoholics and controls in laboratory conditions, *Quarterly Journal of Studies on Alcohol*, **32**, 442–53.

Berne, E. (1964) *Games people play*. New York: Grove Press.

Bigelow, G., Cohen, M., Liebson, I. and Faillace, L. A. (1972) Abstinence or moderation? Choice by alcoholics, *Behaviour Research and Therapy*, **10**, 209–14.

Bigelow, G. and Liebson, I. (1972) Cost factors controlling alcoholic drinking, *Psychological Record*, **22**, 305–14.

The Brewers' Society (1980) *UK statistical handbook 1980*. London: Brewing Publications.

The Brewers' Society (1981) *UK statistical handbook, 1981*. London: Brewing Publications.

Campaign (1980) 2 May, 24–40.

Cautela, J. R. (1970) The treatment of alcoholism by covert sensitization, *Psychotherapy: Theory, Research and Practice*, **7**, 86–90.

Davies, D. L. (1962) Normal drinking in recovered alcohol addicts, *Quarterly Journal of Studies on Alcohol*, **23**, 94–104.

Davies, D. L. and Stacey, B. (1972) *Teenagers and alcohol: a developmental study in Glasgow, Vol. II*. London: HMSO.

Department of the Environment (1976) *Drinking and driving*. Dept. Committee report under the chairmanship of Blennerhassett. London: HMSO.

Donnan, S. and Haskey, J. (1977) Alcoholism and cirrhosis of the liver, *Population Trends*, **7**, 18–24.

Duffy, M. (1981) The influence of prices, consumer incomes and advertising upon the demand for alcoholic drink in the United Kingdom: an econometric study, *British Journal on Alcohol and Alcoholism*, **16**, 200–8.

Edwards, G. (1977) The alcohol dependence syndrome: usefulness of an idea. In G. Edwards and M. Grant (eds), *Alcoholism: new knowledge and new responses*. London: Croom Helm.

Edwards, G., Gross, M. M., Keller, M., Moser, J. and Room, R. (eds) (1977) *Alcohol-related disabilities*. WHO Offset Publication No. 32. Geneva: World Health Organization.

Edwards, G., Hensman, C. and Peto, J. (1971) Drinking problems among recidivist prisoners, *Psychological Medicine*, **5**, 388–99.

Edwards, G., Orford, J., Egert, S., Guthrie, S., Hawker, A., Hernsman, C., Mitcheson, M., Oppenheimer, E. and Taylor, C. (1977) Alcoholism: a controlled trial of 'treatment' and 'advice', *Journal of Studies on Alcohol*. **38**, 1004–30.

Emrick, C. D. (1974) A review of psychologically oriented treatment of alcoholism: I. The use and interrelationship of outcome criteria and drinking behaviour following treatment, *Quarterly Journal of Studies on Alcohol*, **35**, 523–49.

Emrick, C. D. (1975) A review of psychologically oriented treatment of alcoholism. II. The relative effectiveness of different treatment approaches and the effectiveness of treatment versus no treatment, *Journal of Studies on Alcohol*, **36**, 88–108.

Evans, C. M. (1980) Alcohol, violence and aggression, *British*

Journal of Alcohol and Alcoholism, **15**, 104–17.

Ewing, J. A. and Rouse, B. A. (1976) Failure of an experimental treatment program to inculcate controlled drinking in alcoholics, *British Journal of Addiction*, **71**, 123–34.

Federation of Alcoholic Rehabilitation Establishments (1979) *Alcoholism and Alcoholism Services Now*, November.

Fenichel, O. (1945) *The psychoanalytic theory of neurosis*. New York: Norton.

Gerard, D. L., Saenger, G. and Wile, R. (1962) The abstinent alcoholic, *Archives of General Psychiatry*, **6**, 83–95.

Goodwin, D. W., Schulsinger, F., Hermansen, L., Guze, S. B. and Winokur, G. A. (1973) Alcohol problems in adoptees raised apart from alcoholic biological parents, *Archives of General Psychiatry*, **128**, 238–43.

Goodwin, D. W., Schulsinger, F., Knopp, J., Mednick, S. A. and Guze, S. B. (1977) Psychopathology in adopted and non-adopted daughters of alcoholics, *Archives of General Psychiatry*, **34**, 1005–9.

Goodwin, D. W., Schulsinger, F., Moller, N., Hermansen, L., Winokur, G. A. and Guze, S. B. (1974) Drinking problems in adopted and non-adopted sons of alcoholics, *Archives of General Psychiatry*, **31**, 164–9.

Grant, M. (1979) Prevention. In M. Grant and P. Gwinner (eds), *Alcoholism in perspective*. London: Croom Helm.

Hansard. Written answers. Vol. 981, 146, Col. 609, 26.3.1980.

Hansard. Written answers. Vol. 982, 149, Col. 73, 31.3.1980.

Harris, D. (1982) Duty rise will hit drink and tobacco sales. *The Times*, 10 March, p. 7.

Hawker, A. (1978) *Adolescents and alcohol*. London: Edsall.

Health and Safety Executive (1981) *The problem drinker at work*. London: HMSO.

Social Trends, No. 11 (1981) London: HMSO.

Hodgson, R., Rankin, H. and Stockwell, T. (1979) Alcohol dependence and the priming effect, *Behaviour Research and Therapy*, **17**, 379–87.

Holtermann, S. and Burchell, A. (1981) *The cost of alcohol abuse*. Working Paper No. 73. London: Government Economic Service.

Home Office (1979) *Offences of Drunkenness in England and*

Wales, 1978. London: HMSO.

Hunt, G. M. and Azrin, N. H. (1973) A community-reinforcement approach to alcoholism, *Behaviour Research and Therapy,* **11,** 91–104.

Jahoda, G. and Cramond, J. (1972) *Children and alcohol: a developmental study in Glasgow, Vol. 1,* London: HMSO.

Jellinek, E. M. (1952) Phases of alcohol addiction, *Quarterly Journal of Studies on Alcohol,* **13,** 673–84

Jellinek, E. M. (1960) *The disease concept of alcoholism.* New Jersey: Hillhouse Press.

Johnson, L. (1981) Union response to alcoholism, *Journal of Drug Issues,* **11,** 263–77.

Jones, M. C. (1968) Personality correlates and antecedents of drinking patterns in males. *Journal of Consulting and Clinical Psychology,* **32,** 2–12.

Jones, M. C. (1971) Personality antecedents and correlates of drinking patterns in women *Journal of Consulting and Clinical Psychology,* **36,** 61–70.

Keller, M. (1972) On the loss of control phenomenon in alcoholism, *British Journal of Addictions,* **67,** 153–66.

Keller, M. (1977) A lexicon of disablements related to alcohol consumption. In G. Edwards, M. M. Gross, M. Keller, J. Moser and R. Room (eds), *Alcohol-related disabilities.* WHO Offset Publications, No. 32. Geneva: World Health Organization.

Kendell, R. E. (1968) Normal drinking by former alcohol addicts, *Quarterly Journal of Studies on Alcohol,* **24,** 44–60.

Kessel, N. and Walton, H. (1965) *Alcoholism.* Harmondsworth: Penguin Books.

Kilich, S. and Plant, M. A. (1981) Regional variations in the levels of alcohol-related problems in Britian, *British Journal of Addictions,* **76,** 47–62.

Kim, S. (1981) How do we know whether a primary prevention program on drug abuse works or does not work? *International Journal of the Addictions,* **16,** 359–65.

Knight, P. (1937) The psychodynamics of chronic alcoholism, *Journal of Nervous and Mental Diseases,* **86,** 538–48.

Krasner, N. (1977) The reality of medico-psychiatric co-operation. In G. Edwards and M. Grant (eds), *Alcoholism: New knowledge and new responses.* London: Croom Helm.

Lemere, F. (1953) What happens to alcoholics, *American Journal of Psychiatry*, **109**, 674–76.

Lemere, F. and Voetlin, W. L. (1950) An evaluation of the aversion treatment of alcoholism, *Quarterly Journal of Studies on Alcohol*, **11**, 199–204.

Lisansky, E. T. (1974) Alcoholism: the avoided diagnosis, *Bulletin of the American College of Physicians*, **15**, 18–24.

Lloyd, R. W. Jr and Salzberg, H. C. (1975) Controlled social drinking: an alternative to abstinence as a treatment goal for some alcohol abusers, *Psychological Bulletin*, **82**, 815–42.

Lovibond, S. H. and Caddy, G. (1970) Discriminated aversive control in the moderation of alcoholics' drinking behavior, *Behavior Therapy*, **1**, 437–44.

Marlatt, G. A., Denning, B. and Reid, J. B. (1973) Loss of control drinking in alcoholics: an experimental analogue, *Journal of Abnormal Psychology*, **81**, 233–41.

Maynard, A. and Kennan, P. (1981) The economics of alcohol abuse, *British Journal of Addiction*, **76**, 339–45.

Mello, N. K. (1972) Behavioral studies of alcoholism. In B. Kissin and H. Begleiter (eds), *The biology of alcoholism, Vol. 2*. New York: Plenum.

Mendelson, J. H., LaDou, L. and Solomon, P. (1964) Experimentally induced chronic intoxication and withdrawal in alcoholics. Part 3: Psychiatric findings, *Quarterly Journal of Studies on Alcohol*, **40**, suppl. 2.

Miller, P. M. (1976) *Behavioural treatment of alcoholism*. Oxford: Pergamon.

Miller, P. M. and Foy, D. W. (1981) Substance abuse. In S. M. Turner, K. S. Cahoun and H. E. Adams (eds), *Handbook of clinical behavior therapy*. New York: Wiley.

Miller, W. R. and Caddy, G. R. (1977) Abstinence and controlled drinking in the treatment of problem drinkers, *Journal of Studies on Alcohol*, **38**, 986–1003.

Miller, W. R., Gribskov, C. J. and Mortell, R. L. (1981) Effectiveness of a self-control manual for problem drinkers with and without therapist contact, *International Journal of the Addictions*, **16**, 1247–54.

Mills, K. C., Sobell, M. B. and Schaefer, H. H. (1971) Training social drinking as an alternative to abstinence for alcoholics, *Behavior Therapy*, **2**, 18–27.

McClelland, D. C., Davis, W. N., Kalin, R. and Warner, E.

(1972) *The drinking man*. New York: Free Press.

McCord, W., McCord, J. and Gudeman, J. (1960) *Origins of alcoholism*. Stanford, California: Stanford University Press.

Nagarajam, M., Gross, M. M., Kissin, B. and Best, S. (1973) Affective changes during 6 days of experimental alcoholization and subsequent withdrawal. In M. M. Gross (ed), *Alcohol intoxication and withdrawal: Experimental studies I*. New York: Plenum.

Nathan, P. E. and O'Brien, J. S. (1971) An experimental analysis of the behavior of alcoholics and non-alcoholics during prolonged experimental drinking: A necessary precursor of behavior therapy? *Behavior Therapy*, **2**, 455–76.

Office of Health Economics (1981) *Alcohol: reducing the harm*. London: Office of Health Economics.

Ogborne, A. C. and Glaser, F. B. (1981) Characteristics of affiliates of Alcoholics Anonymous: a review of the literature, *Journal of Studies on Alcohol*, **42**, 661–75.

Ogborne, A. C. and Smart, G. (1980) Will restrictions on alcohol advertising reduce alcohol consumption? *British Journal of Addictions*, **75**, 293–6.

Paredes, A. (1974) Denial, deceptive maneuvers and consistency in the behavior of alcoholics, *Annals of the New York Academy of Science*, **233**, 23–33.

Pattison, M. (1976) Nonabstinent drinking goals in the treatment of alcoholism: a clinical typology, *Archives of General Psychiatry*, **33**, 923–30.

Pollack, D. (1965) *Experimental intoxication of alcoholics and normals: some psychological changes*. Doctoral dissertation, University of California.

Popham, R. E., Schmidt, W. and de Lint, J. (1975) The prevention of alcoholism: epidemiological studies of the effects of government control measures, *British Journal of Addictions*, **70**, 125–44.

Registrar General (1975) *Diennial Supplement, England and Wales, 1951, part 2*. London: HMSO.

Roman, P. M. (1981) From employee alcoholism to employee assistance: de-emphases on prevention and alcohol problems in work-based programs, *Journal of Studies on Alcohol*, **42**, 244–72.

Roueche, B. (1960) *Alcohol: its history, folklore, effect on the human body*. New York: Grove.

Royal College of Psychiatrists (1979) *Alcohol and Alcoholism. The report of a Special Committee of the Royal College of Psychiatrists*. London: Tavistock.

Ruprecht, A. Alcoholism, denial and the physician (1970) *Postgraduate Medicine*, **47**, 165–71.

Saunders, J. B., Davis, M. and Williams, R. (1981) Do women develop alcoholic liver disease more readily than men? *British Medical Journal*, **282**, 1140–43.

Silverstein, S. J., Nathan, P. E. and Taylor, H. A. (1974) Blood alcohol level estimation and controlled drinking by chronic alcoholics, *Behavior Therapy*, **5**, 1–15.

Smith, R. (1981a) The relation between consumption and damage, *British Medical Journal*, **283**, 895–8.

Smith, R. (1981b) Preventing alcohol problems: a job for Canute? *British Medical Journal*, **283**, 972–4.

Sobell, M. B. and Sobell, L. C. (1973a) Individualized behavior therapy for alcoholics. *Behavior Therapy*, **4**, 49–72.

Sobell, M. B. and Sobell, L. C. (1973b) Alcoholics treated by individualized behavior therapy: one year treatment outcome, *Behaviour Research and Therapy*, **11**, 599–618.

Sobell, M. B. and Sobell, L. C. (1976) Second year treatment outcome of alcoholics treated by individualized behavior therapy: results, *Behaviour Research and Therapy*, **14**, 195–215.

Tournier, R. E. (1979) Alcoholics Anonymous as treatment and as ideology, *Journal of Studies on Alcohol*, **40**, 230–9.

Trevelyan, G. M. (1944) *English Social History*. London: Longman.

Tuchfeld, B. S. (1981) Spontaneous remission in alcoholics: empirical observations and theoretical implications, *Journal of Studies on Alcohol*, **42**, 626–41.

Vanderpool, J. A. (1969) Alcoholism and the self-concept. *Quarterly Journal of Studies on Alcohol*, **30**, 59–77.

Victor, M. (1975) Polyneuropathy due to nutritional deficiency and alcoholism. In P. J. Dyck, P. K. Thomas and E. H. Lambert (eds), *Peripheral neuropathy*. Philadelphia: Saunders.

Voegtlin, W. L. and Broz, W. R. (1949) The conditional reflex treatment of chronic alcoholism: X. An analysis of 3,125 admissions over a period of ten and a half years, *Annals of Internal Medicine*, **30**, 580–97.

Wilkins, R. H. (1974) *The hidden alcoholic in general practice*. London: Elek Science.

Willett, W., Hennekers, C. H., Siegel, A. J., Adner, M. M. and Castelli, W. P. (1980) Alcohol consumption and high-density lipoprotein cholesterol in marathon runners. *The New England Journal of Medicine*, **303**, 1159–61.

Williams, A. F. (1964) Self-concepts of college problem drinkers, *Quarterly Journal of Studies on Alcohol*, **26**, 586–94.

Williams, Sir W. J. (1976) *Moriarty's Police Law* (23rd edn). London: Butterworth.

Wilson, P. (1980a) *Drinking in England and Wales. An enquiry carried out on behalf of the Department of Health and Social Security*. London: HMSO.

Wilson, P. (1980b) *Population Trends*, **22**, 14–18.

World Health Organization (1952) *Expert Committee on Mental Health. Alcohol Sub-Committee Second Report. Technical Report Series, No. 48*. Geneva: World Health Organization.

World Health Organization (1964) *Expert Committee on Addiction Producing Drugs, Thirteenth Report. WHO Technical report series, No. 273*. Geneva: World Health Organization.

Index